TESSELLATION TEACHING MASTERS

Dale Seymour

DALE SEYMOUR PUBLICATIONS

Dedicated to the late Col. Robert S. Beard,
a good friend who loved making geometric drawings,
born too soon to enjoy the Macintosh computer
and Adobe Illustrator 88.

Cover design: Rachel Gage

Order number DS07900
ISBN 0-86651-462-7

DALE
SEYMOUR
PUBLICATIONS
P.O. BOX 10888
PALO ALTO, CA 94303

14 15 16 17 18 19 20-ML- 04 03 02 01 00

CONTENTS

Introduction *5*

Tessellations of Regular Polygons *7*

Sample Tessellations of Triangles, Quadrilaterals, and Special Hexagons *21*

Semiregular Tessellations *95*

Sample Tessellations of Regular Polygons with Two or More Vertices *113*

Sample Tessellations of Star Polygons *129*

Sample Tessellations of Single Polygonal Shapes *149*

Sample Tessellations of Multiple Polygonal Shapes *173*

Sample Tessellations in Islamic Art *207*

Dual Tessellations *217*

Sample Tessellations of Polyominoes and Letters *227*

Sample Tessellations of Non-Polygons *243*

Sketching Grids for Creating Tessellations *261*

Worksheets and Templates *279*

INTRODUCTION

This book of tessellation designs is a resource for the teacher or student of geometric patterns. It is the companion to *Introduction to Tessellations* by Dale Seymour and Jill Britton (Palo Alto, Calif: Dale Seymour Publications, 1989), a book that introduces the fundamental properties of plane tessellations and demonstrates, step by step, how to create these beautiful tilings or mosaics.

For centuries, artists of almost every culture have used the design properties of pattern in many different art forms. Probably the most outstanding examples of tessellations are found in Islamic art, particularly from the period 700–1500, and in the modern work of Dutch artist M. C. Escher. The experience of tessellating a plane surface can be enjoyed by people of all ages. Children as young as three and four, playing with pattern blocks, create tessellations as they discover how the brightly colored shapes fit together in regular patterns. Older students can begin to understand the principles of this tiling, and for more advanced students, analyzing and designing tessellations of particular types can offer a rigorous intellectual challenge.

In the field of art, people are accustomed to exploring with creative freedom; unfortunately, this has not been the case in the study of mathematics. Too many people view mathematics as a subject filled with rules to be first memorized, then applied. The study of mathematics is so much more interesting when we have the chance to discover patterns and relationships on our own, and when we enjoy the freedom to hypothesize, to experiment, and to verify our conjectures. Analyzing and designing tessellations offers us the opportunity to apply the basic principles of geometry in a problem-solving setting; as we use our critical thinking skills in combination with artistic exploration, we can discover fascinating new relationships.

The tessellation teaching masters in this book can be used in a number of ways. You might reproduce individual pages on acetate, making overhead transparencies to present examples of certain classifications of tessellations and to illustrate their properties. Some of the designs have been prepared in an enlarged format specifically for use as transparencies. You can also photocopy any of the pages as worksheets for classifying, creating, and analyzing the designs. A variety of sketching grids and other materials for designing regular or semiregular tessellations are provided in the last sections of this book. You might photocopy the illustrations of regular polygons onto manila tagboard, then cut out the shapes with an artist's knife to make a template for use in drawing designs. Refer to *Introduction to Tessellations* for specific activity ideas.

This book presents a wide variety of designs, but the offering is by no means complete. For a more comprehensive and advanced treatment of the subject of tessellations, see *Tilings and Patterns* by Branko Grünbaum and G. C. Shephard (New York: W. H. Freeman and Company, 1987).

TESSELLATIONS OF REGULAR POLYGONS

9

11

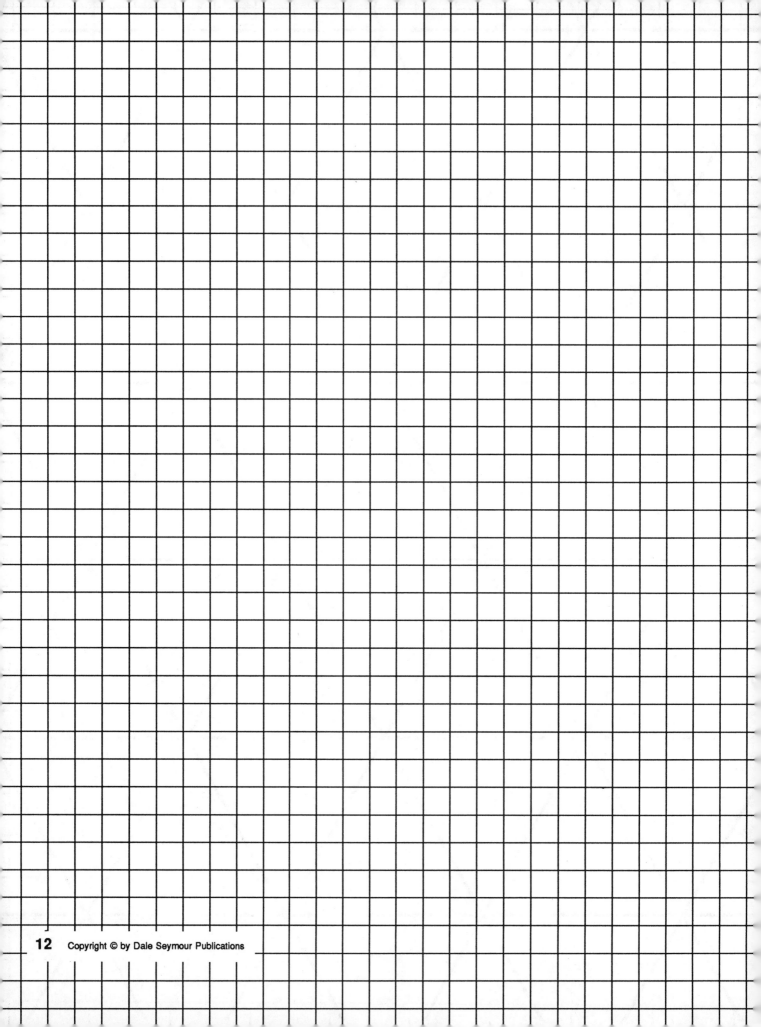

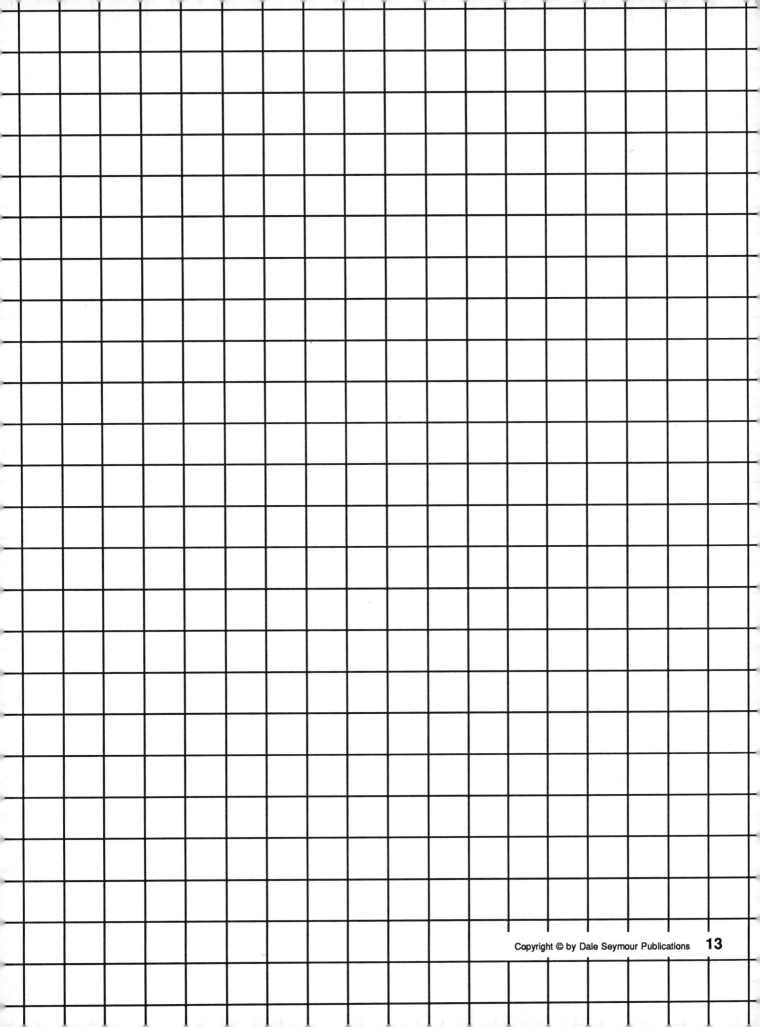

13

15

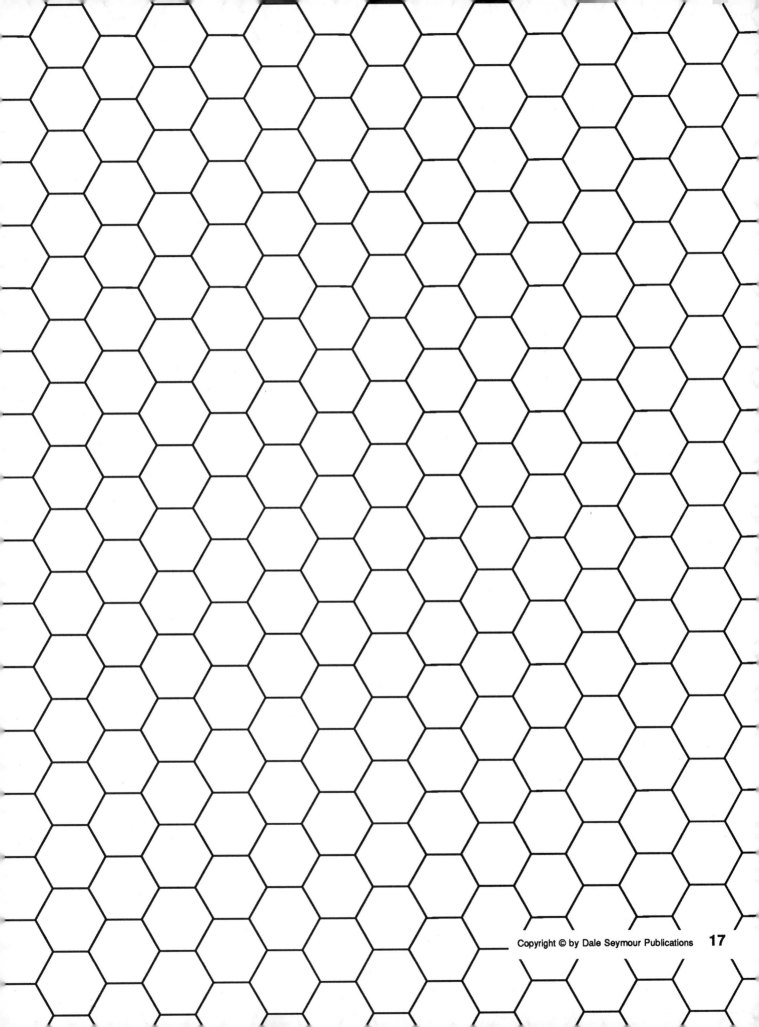

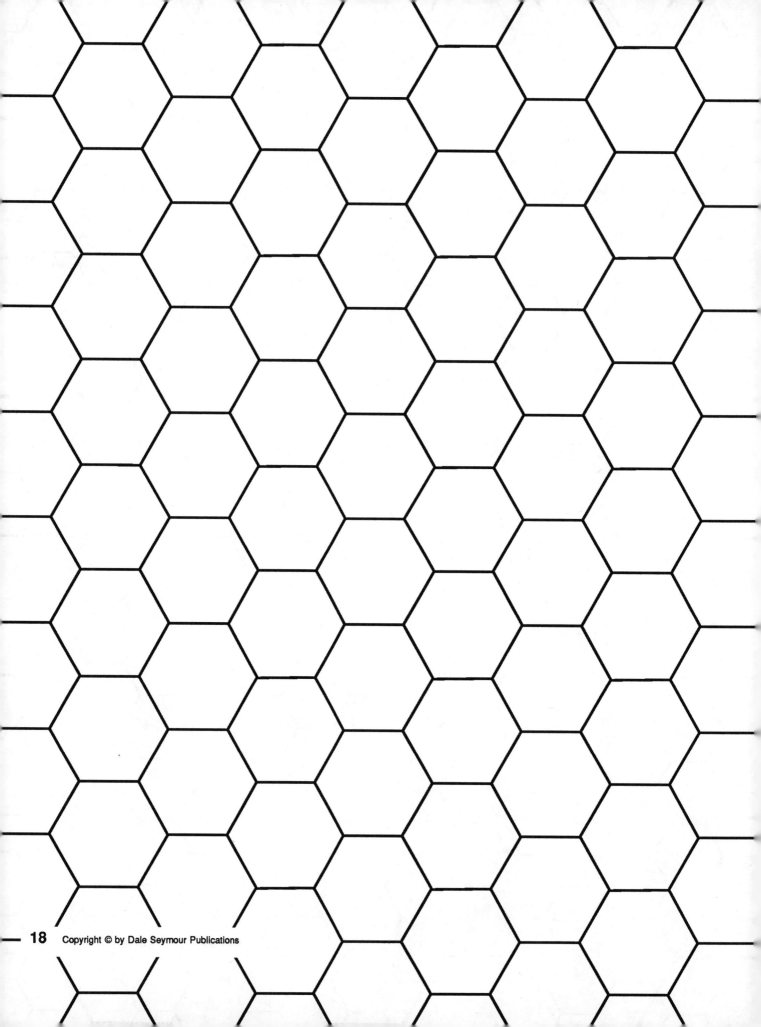

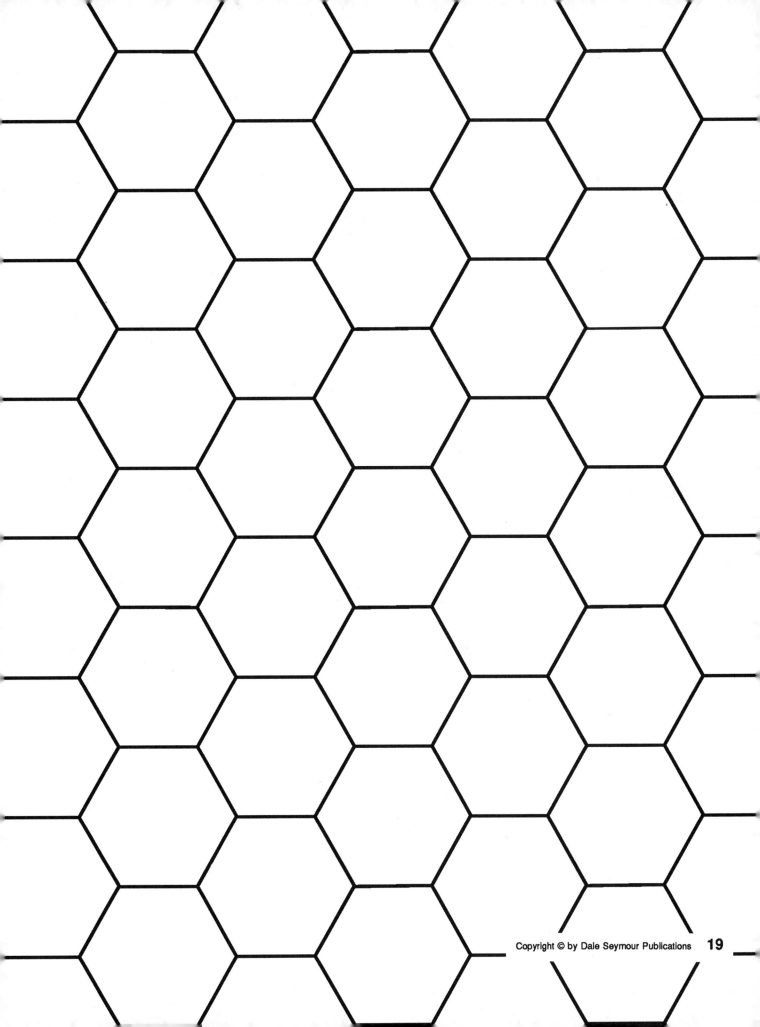

19

REGULAR TESSELLATIONS

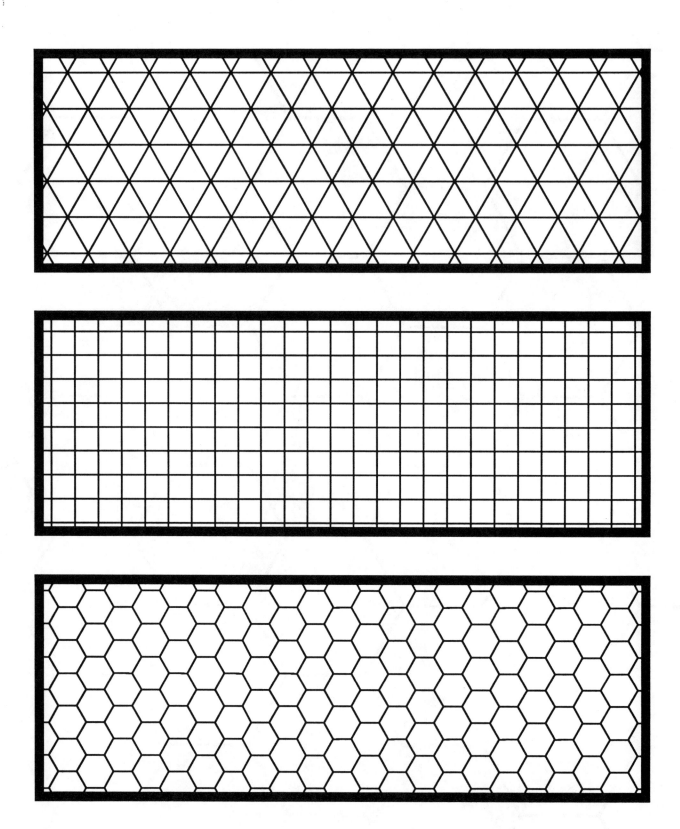

SAMPLE TESSELLATIONS OF TRIANGLES, QUADRILATERALS, AND SPECIAL HEXAGONS

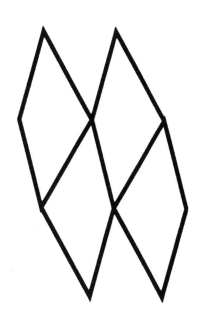

23

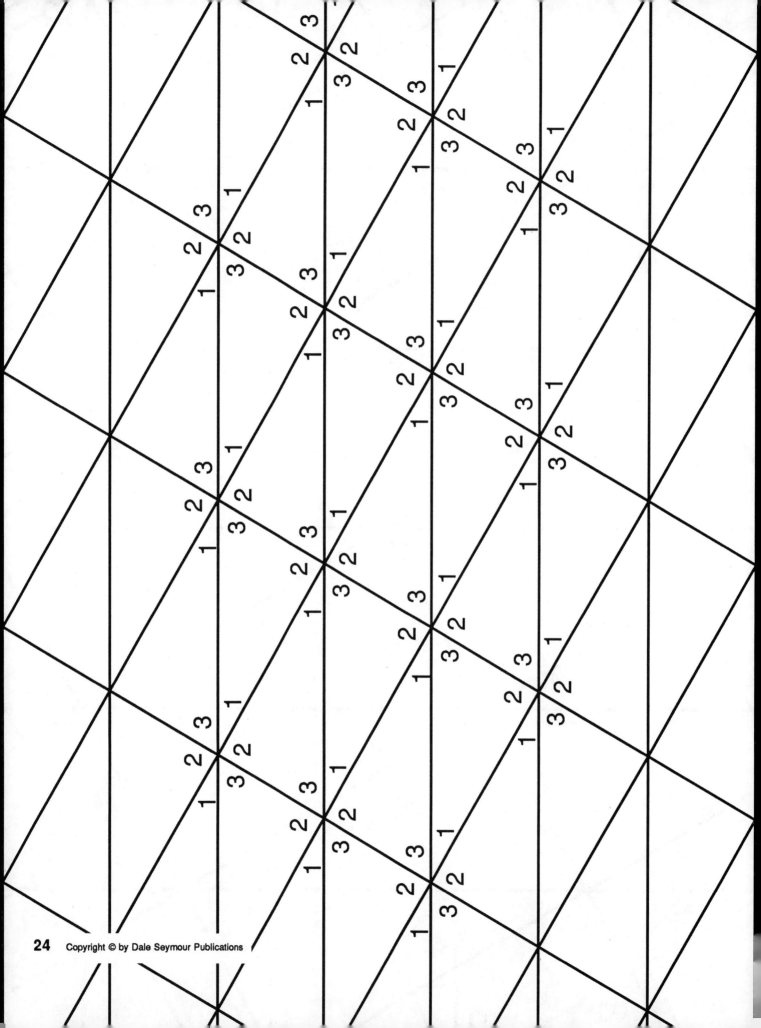

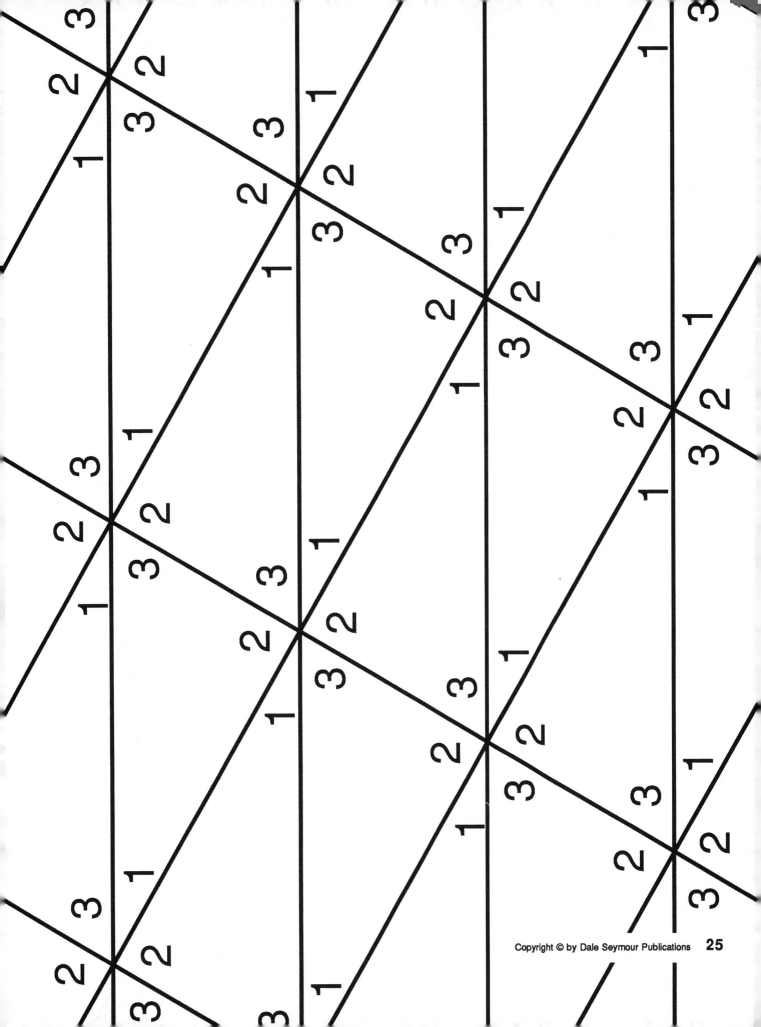

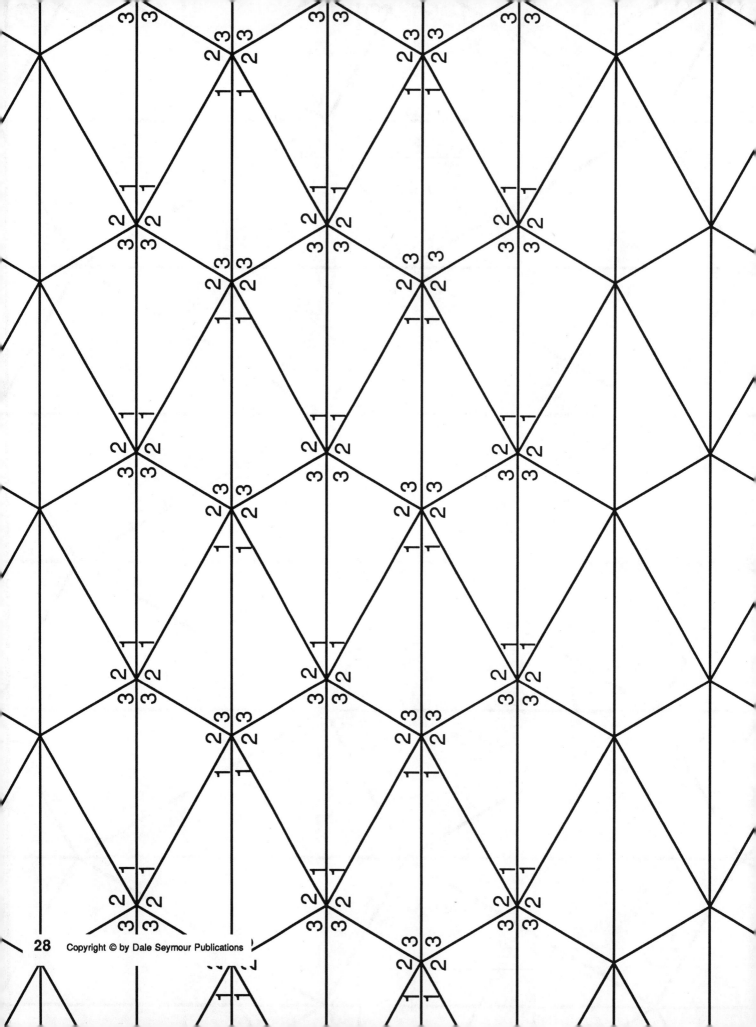

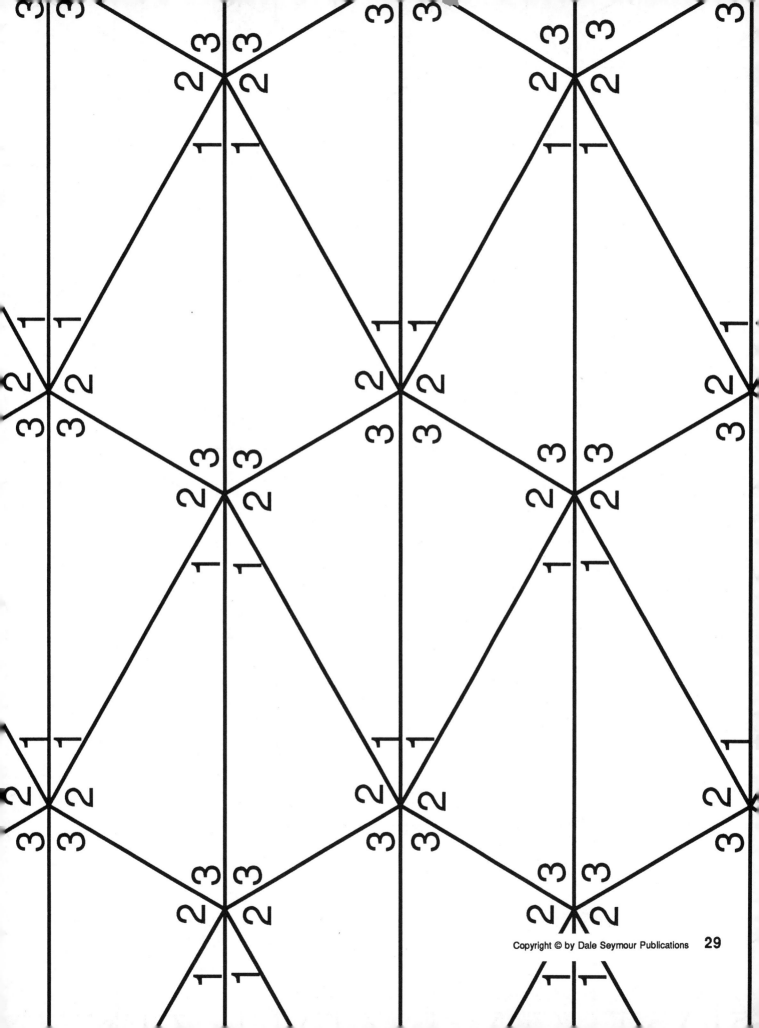

29

31

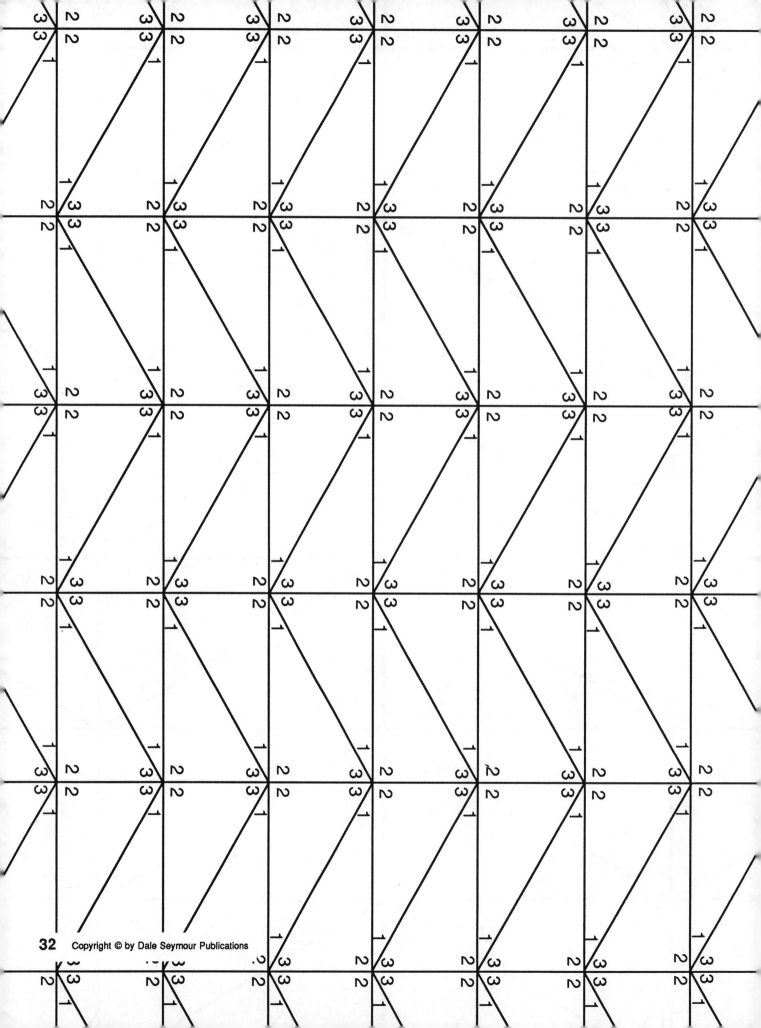

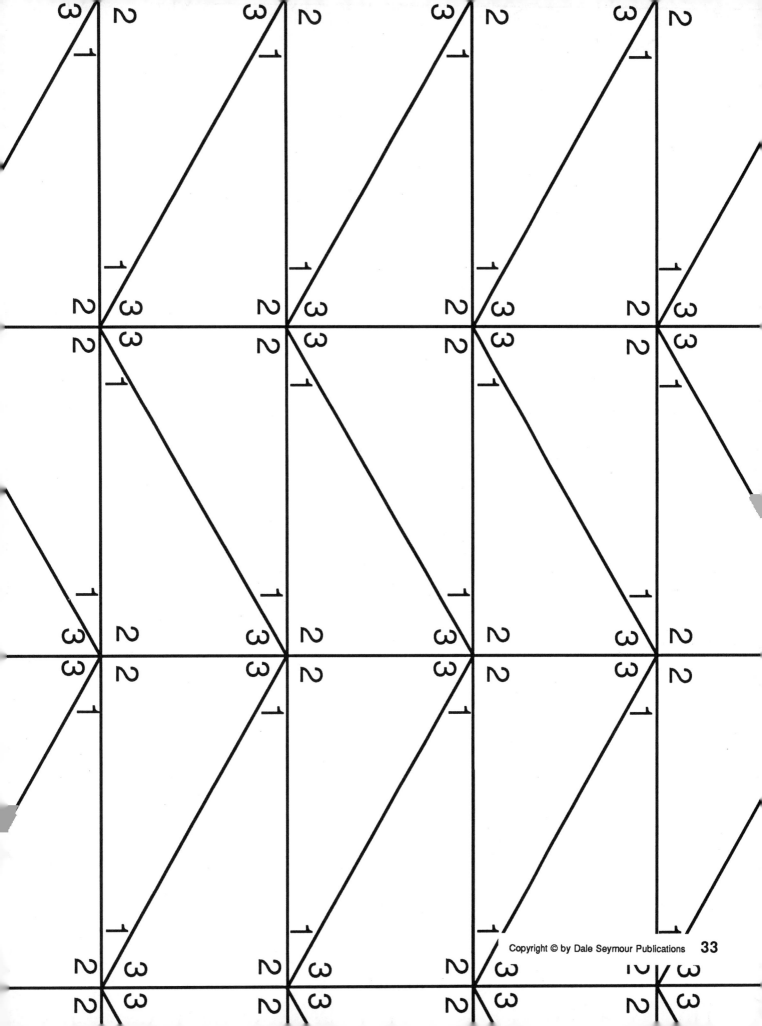

33

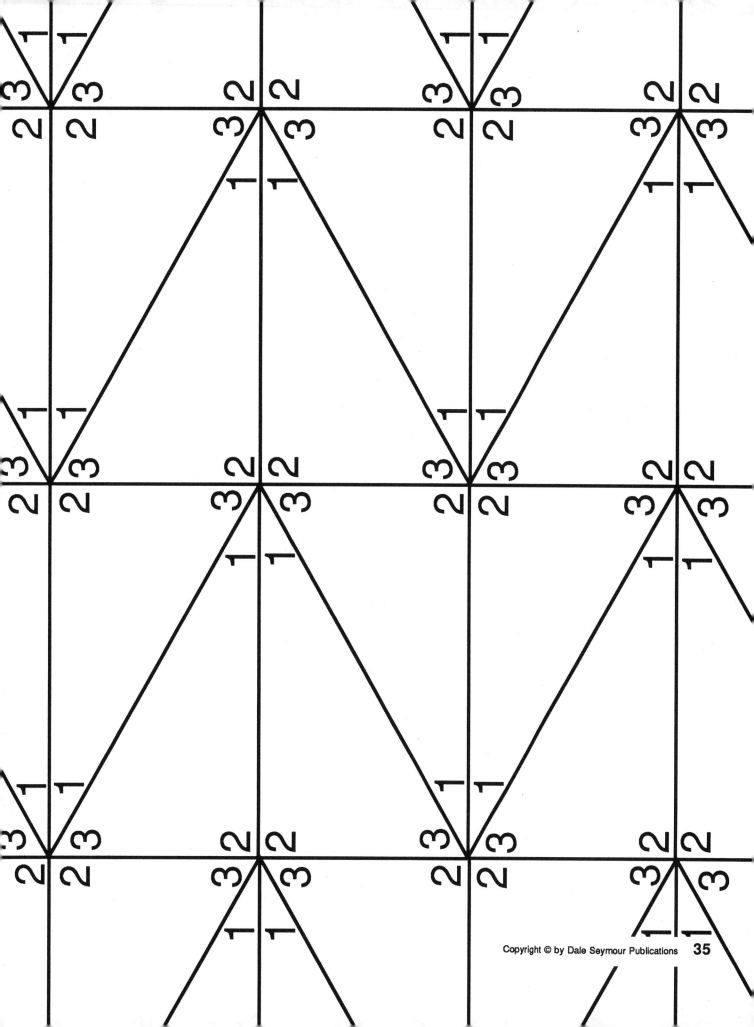

35

37

41

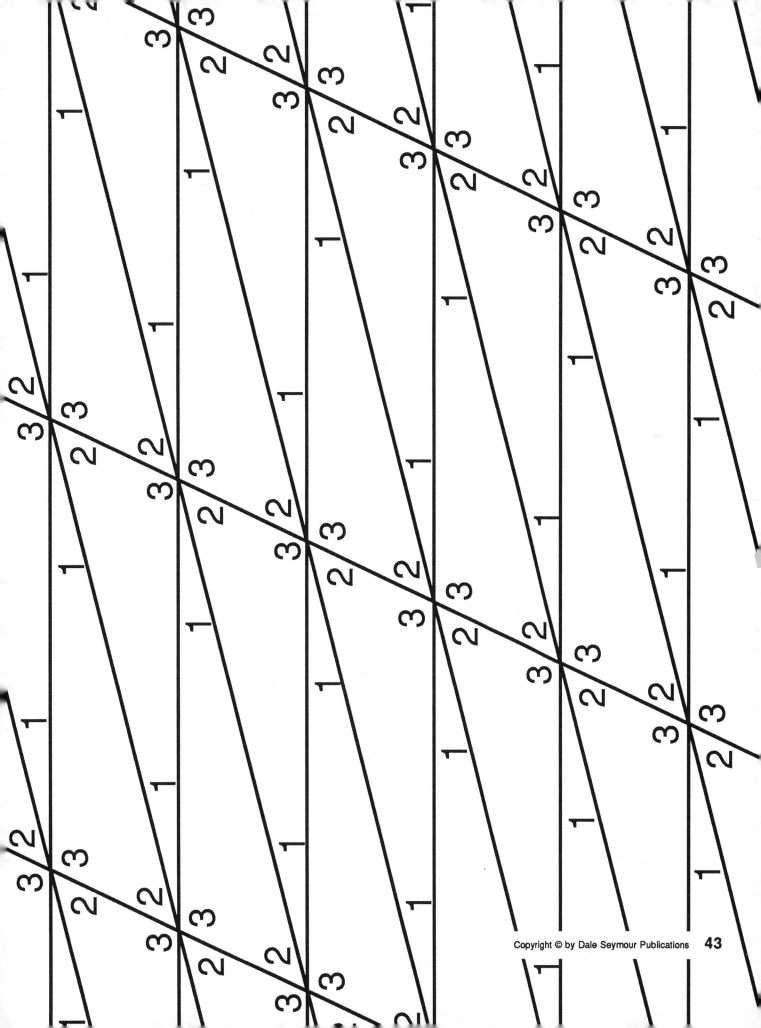

43

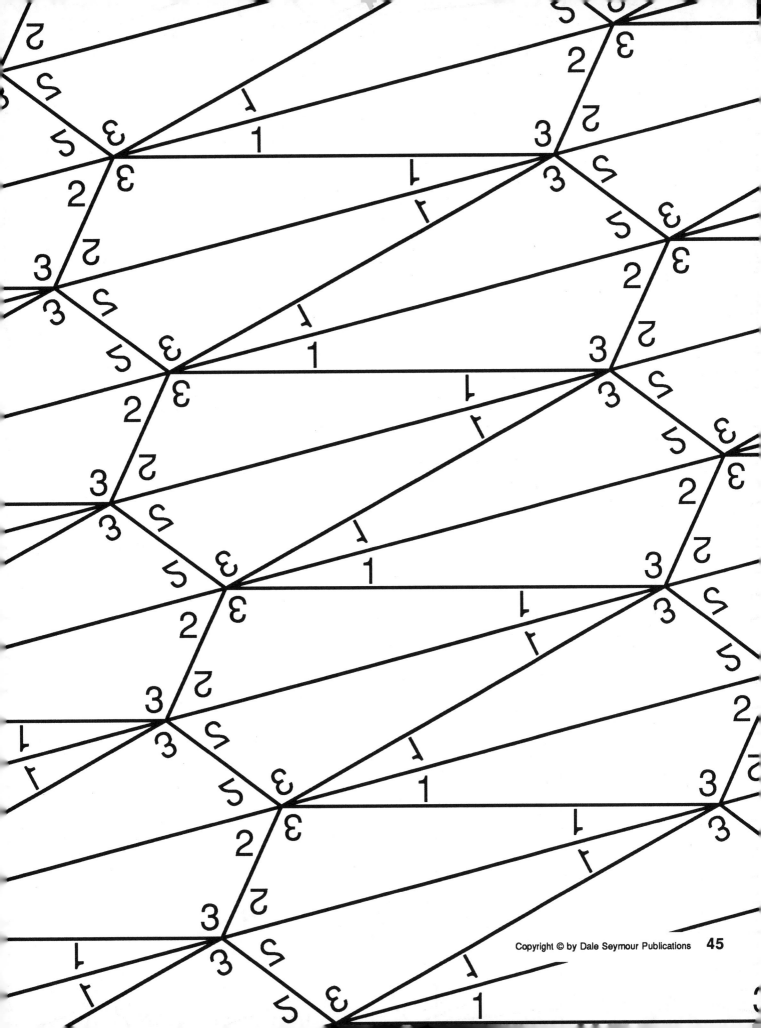

45

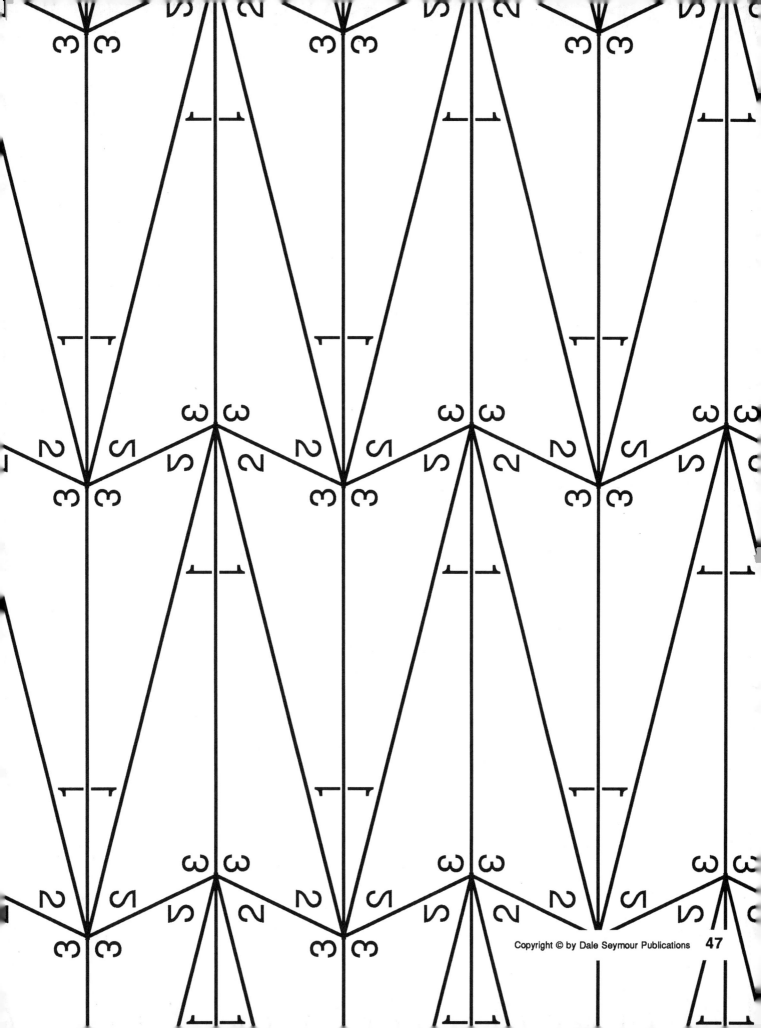

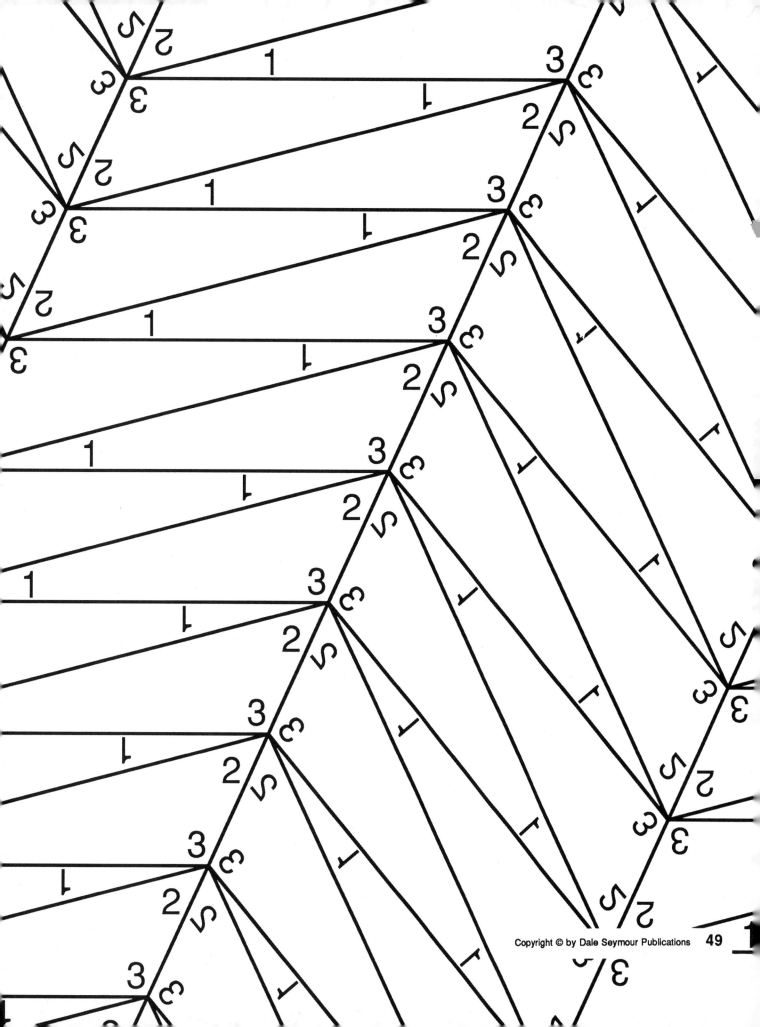

49

TESSELLATION COMBINATIONS

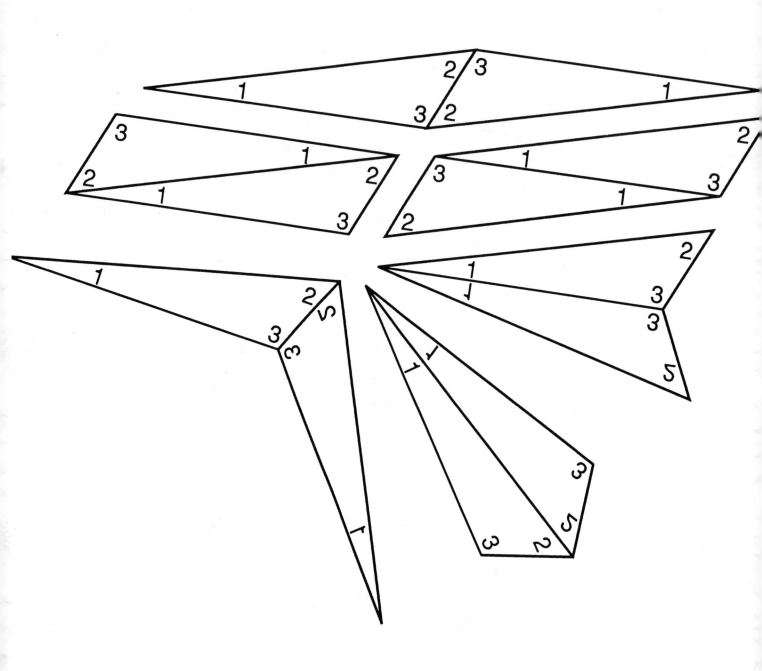

51

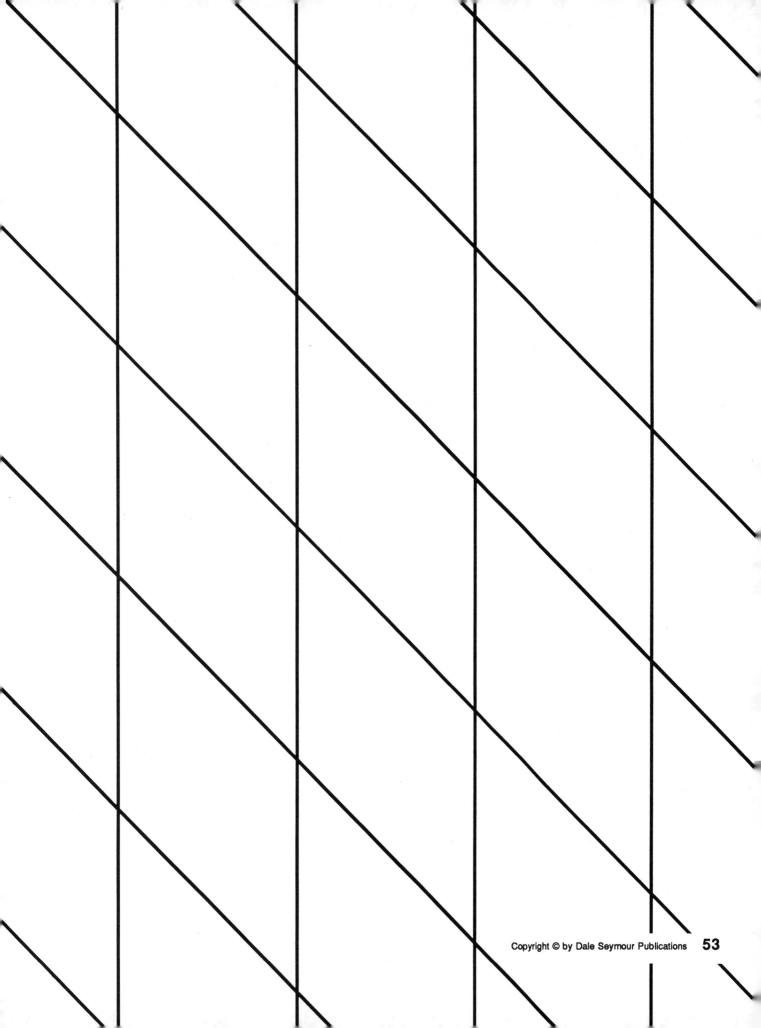

53

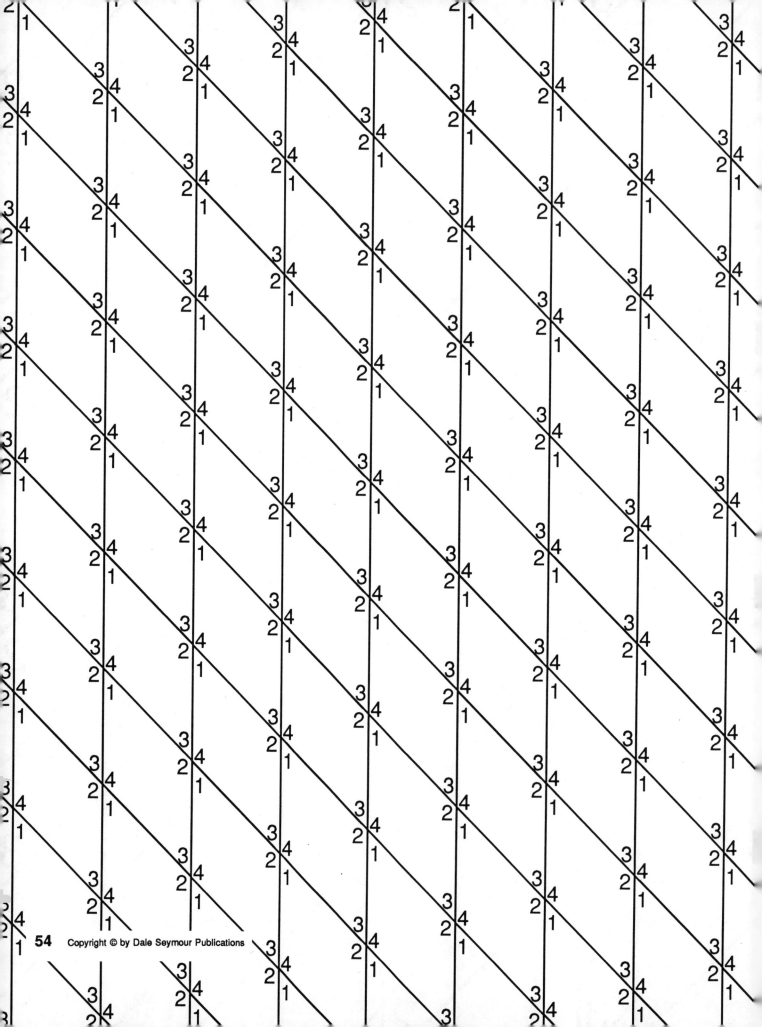

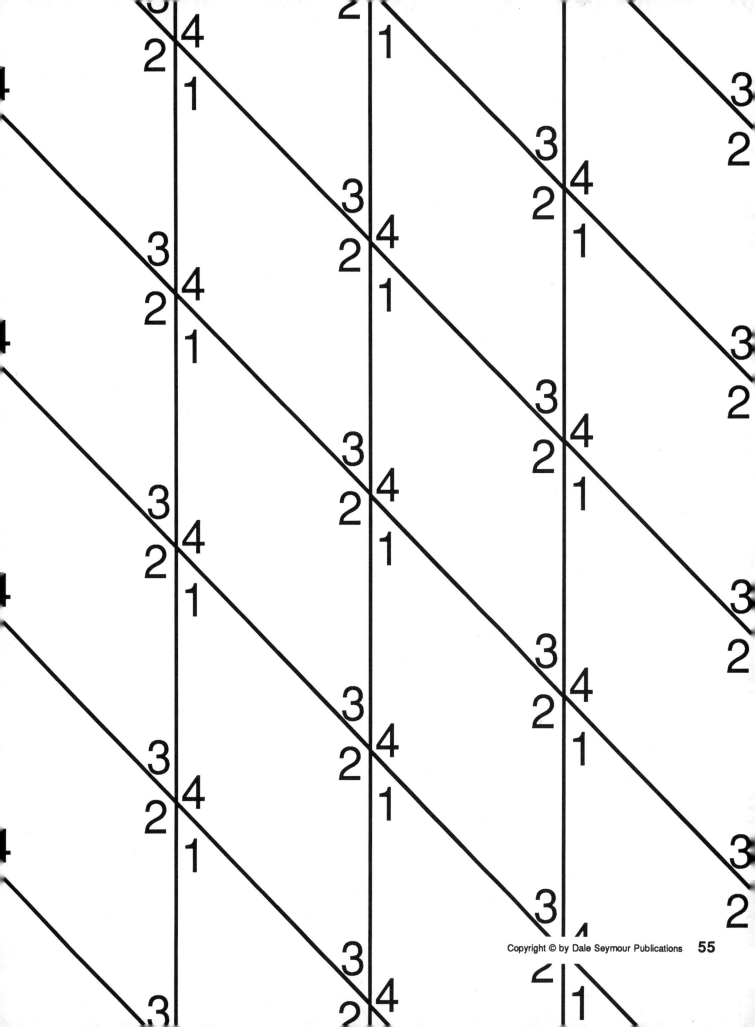

55

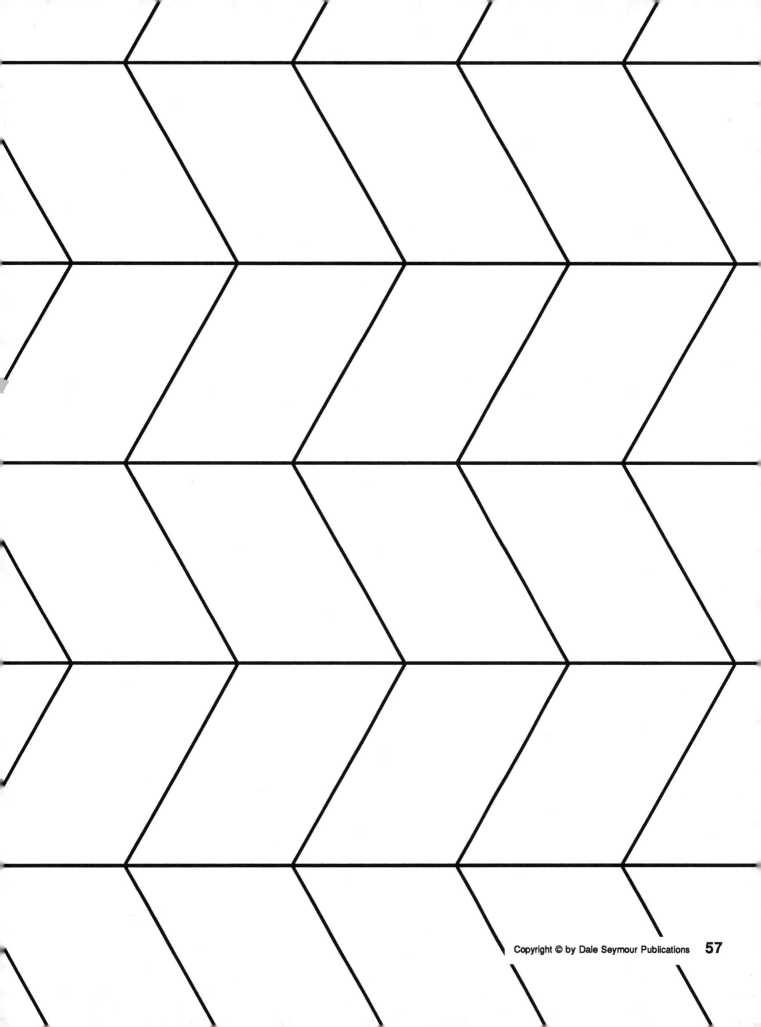

57

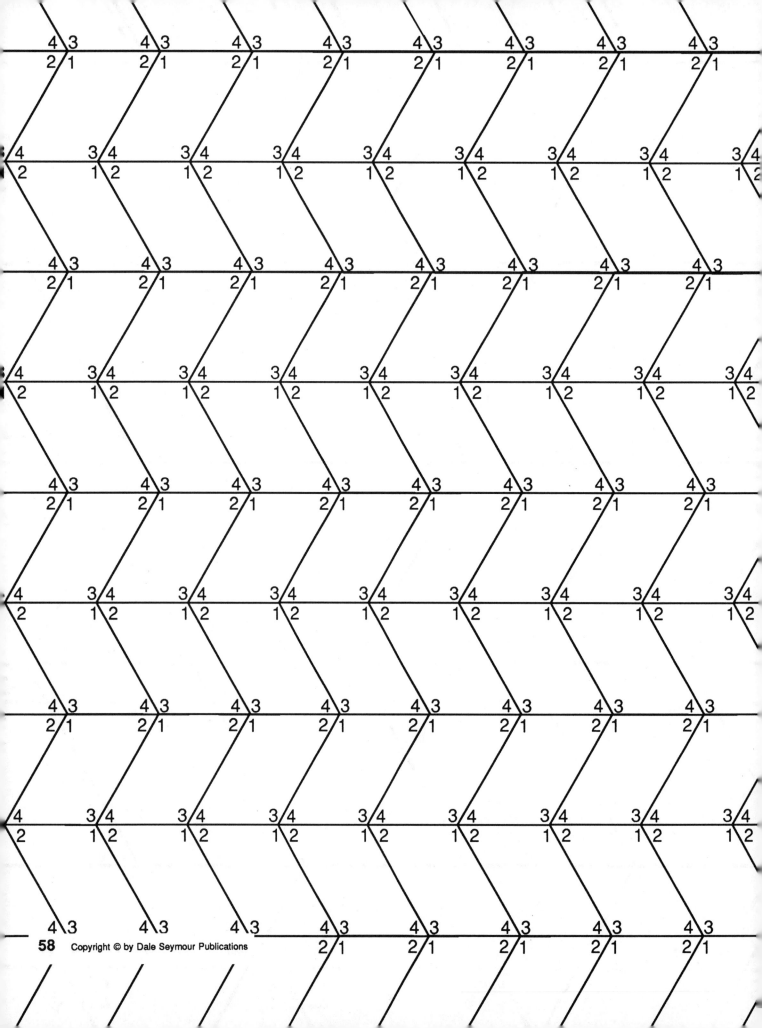

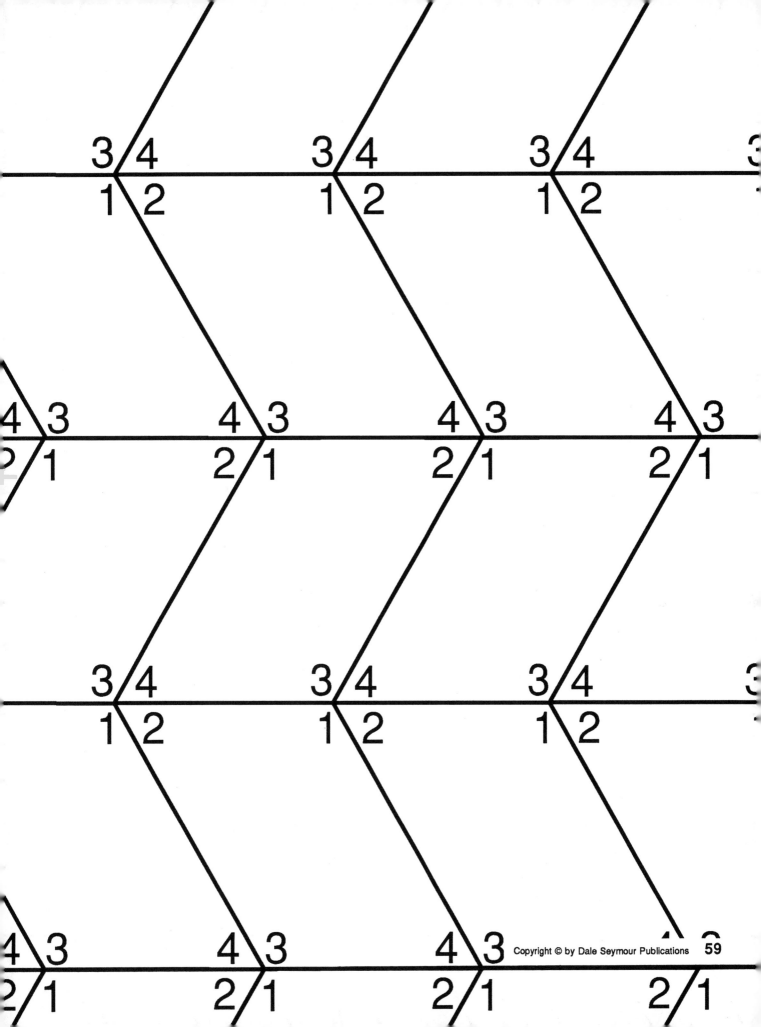

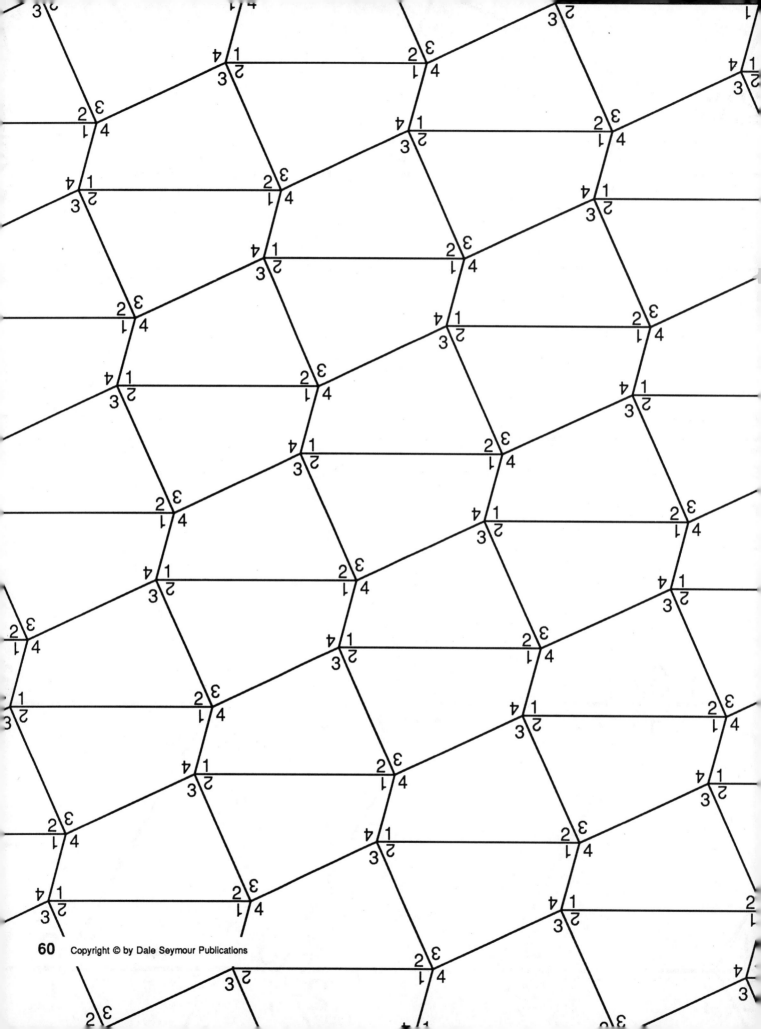

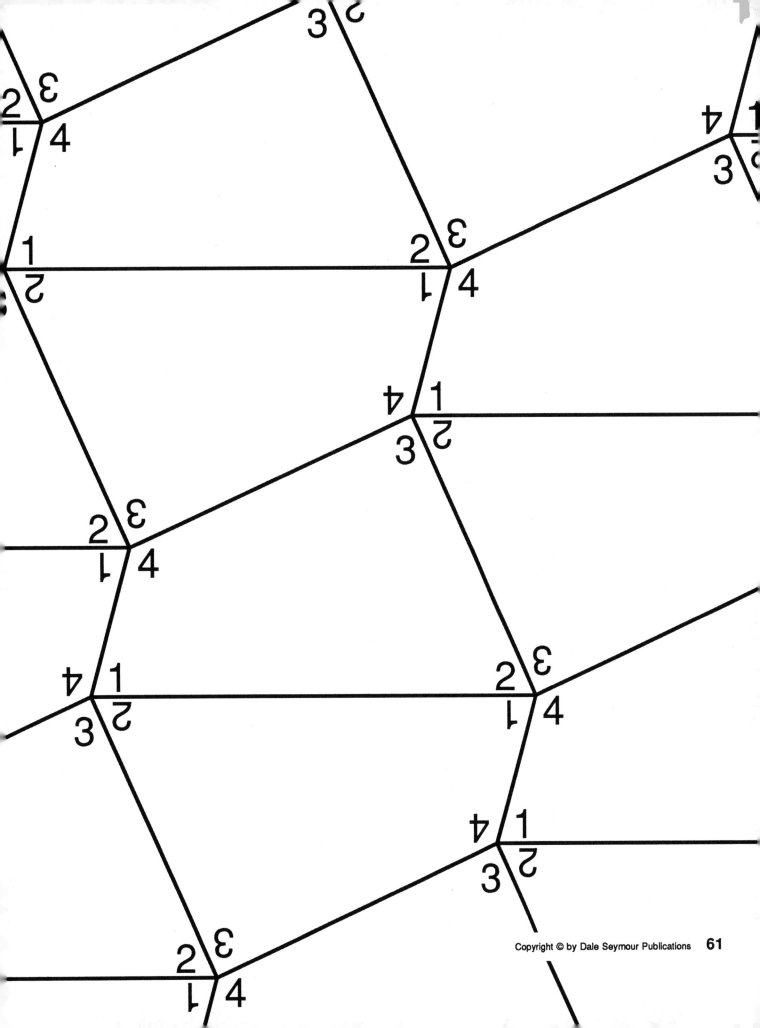

61

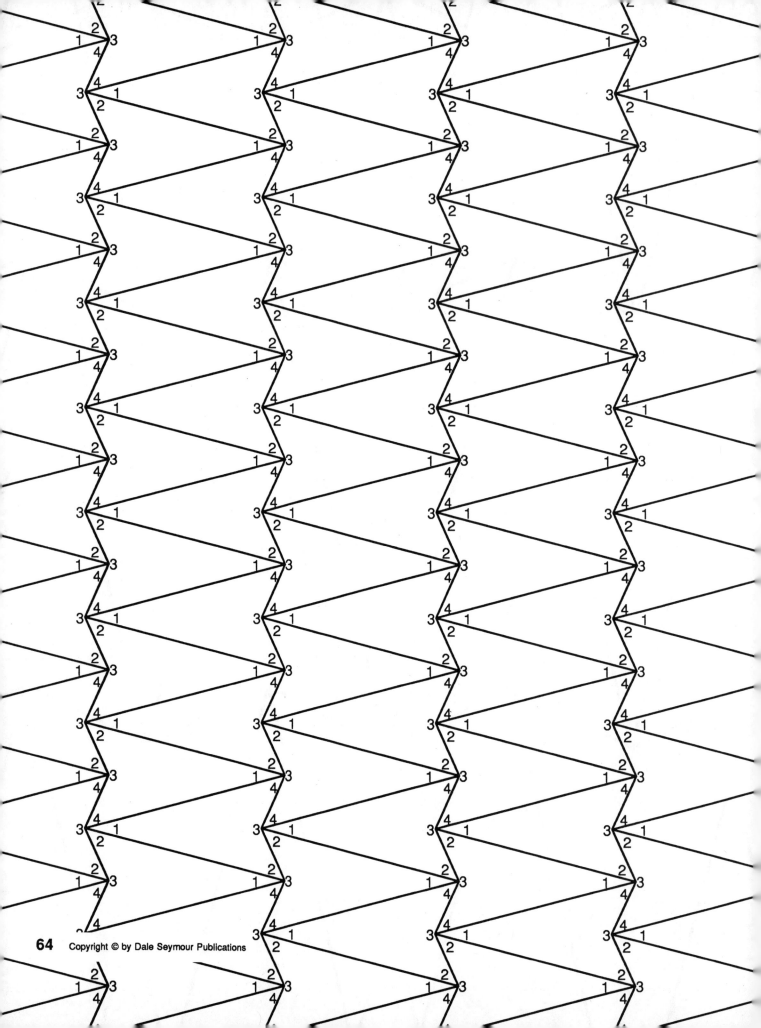

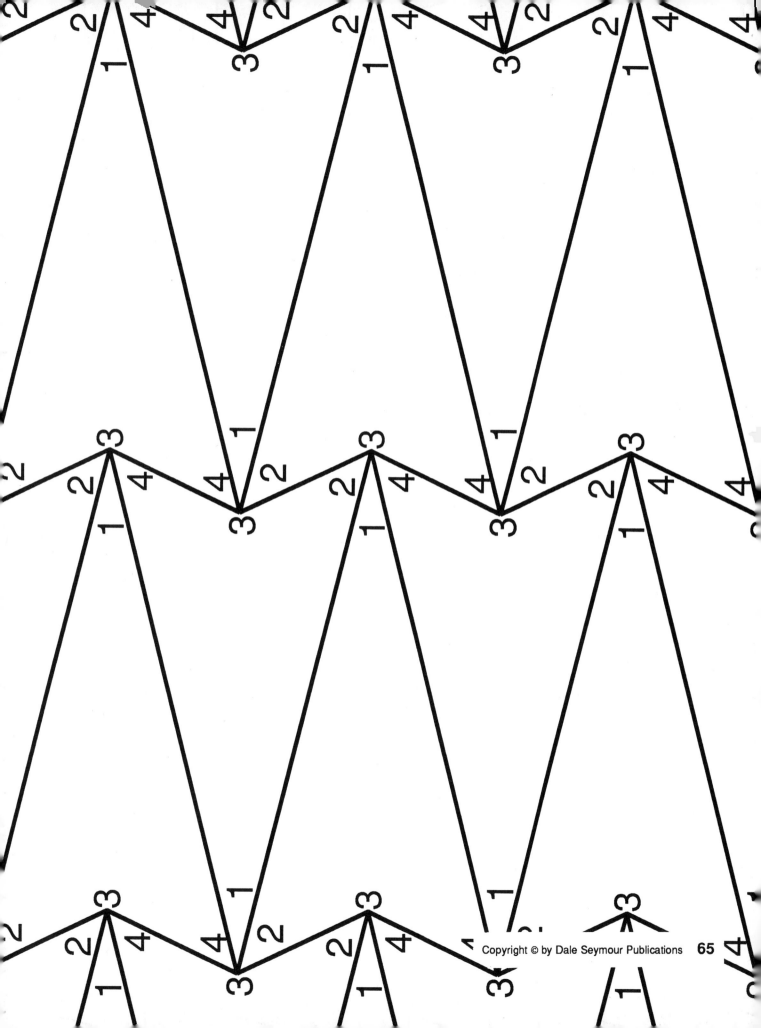

65

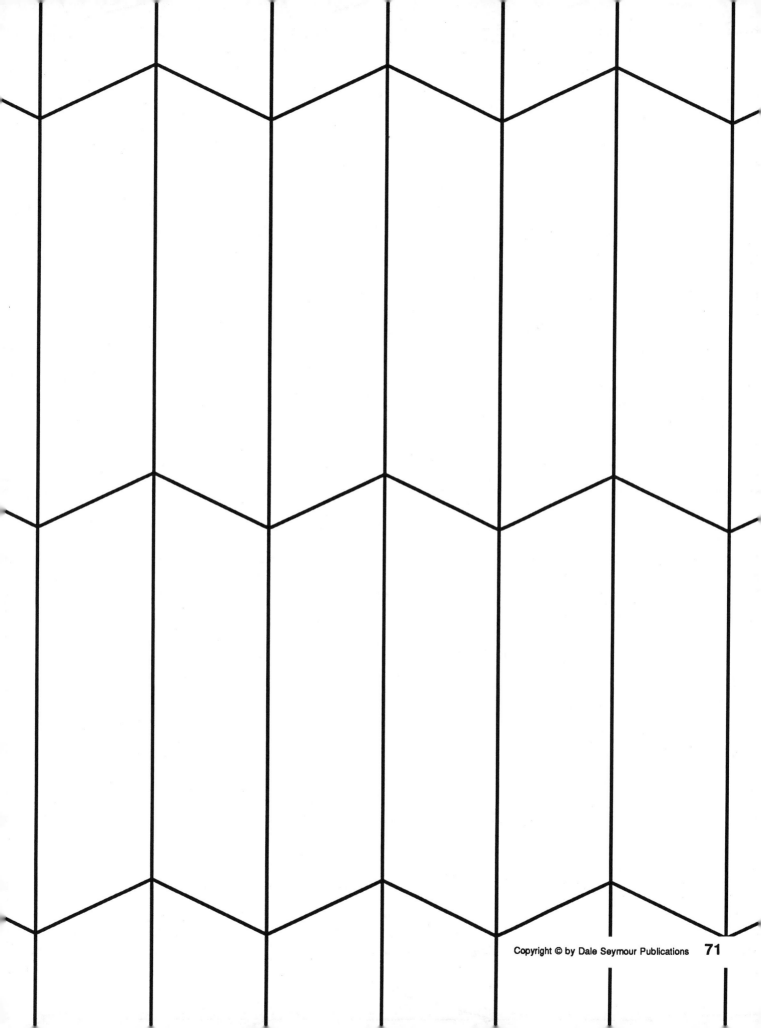

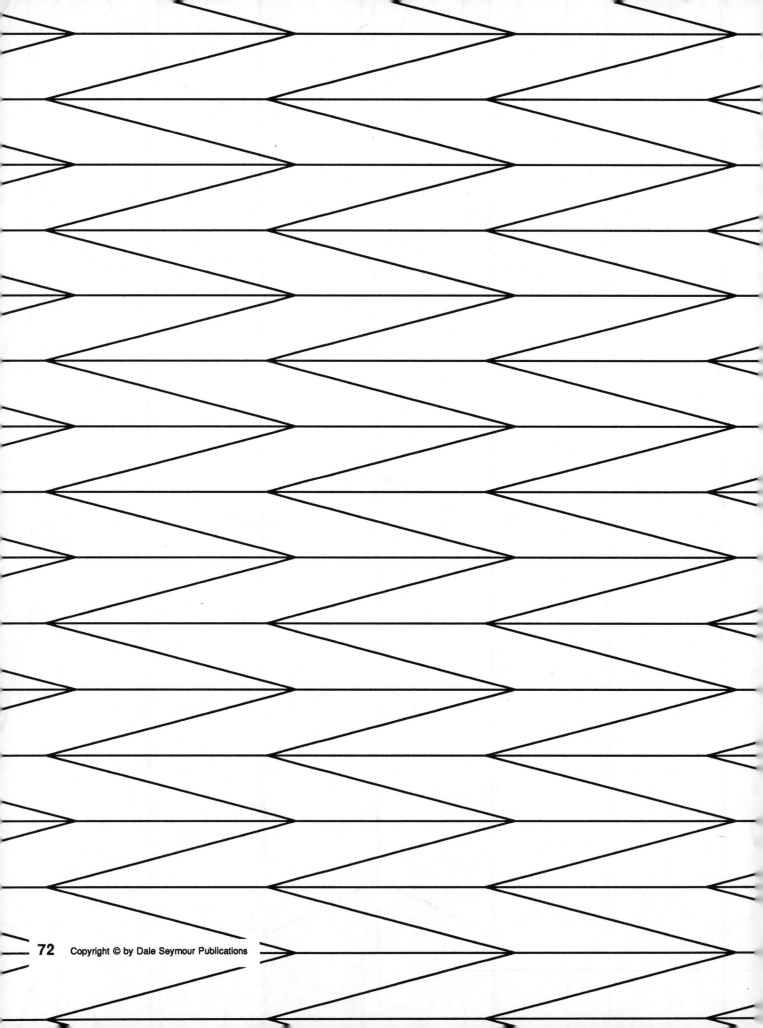

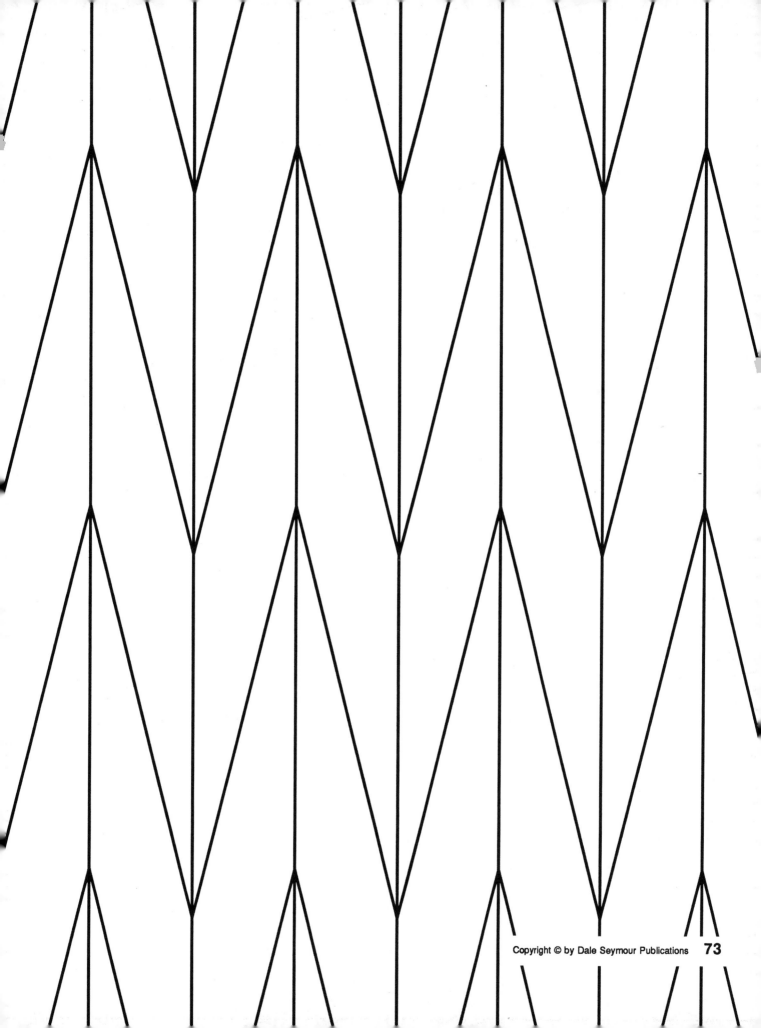

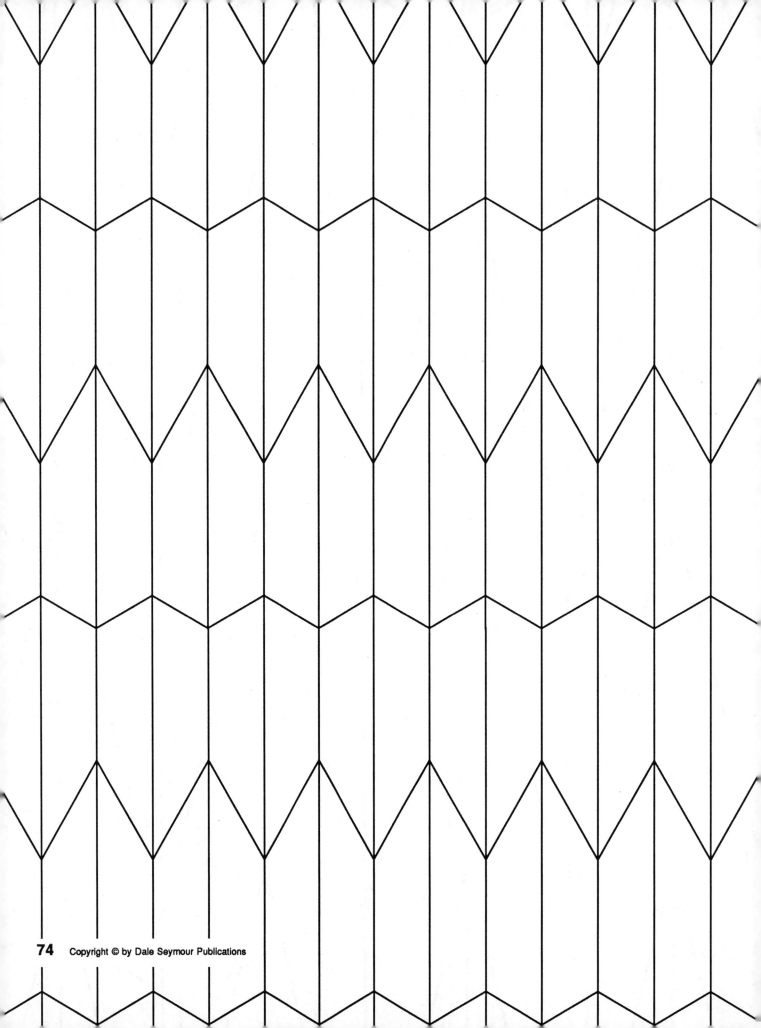

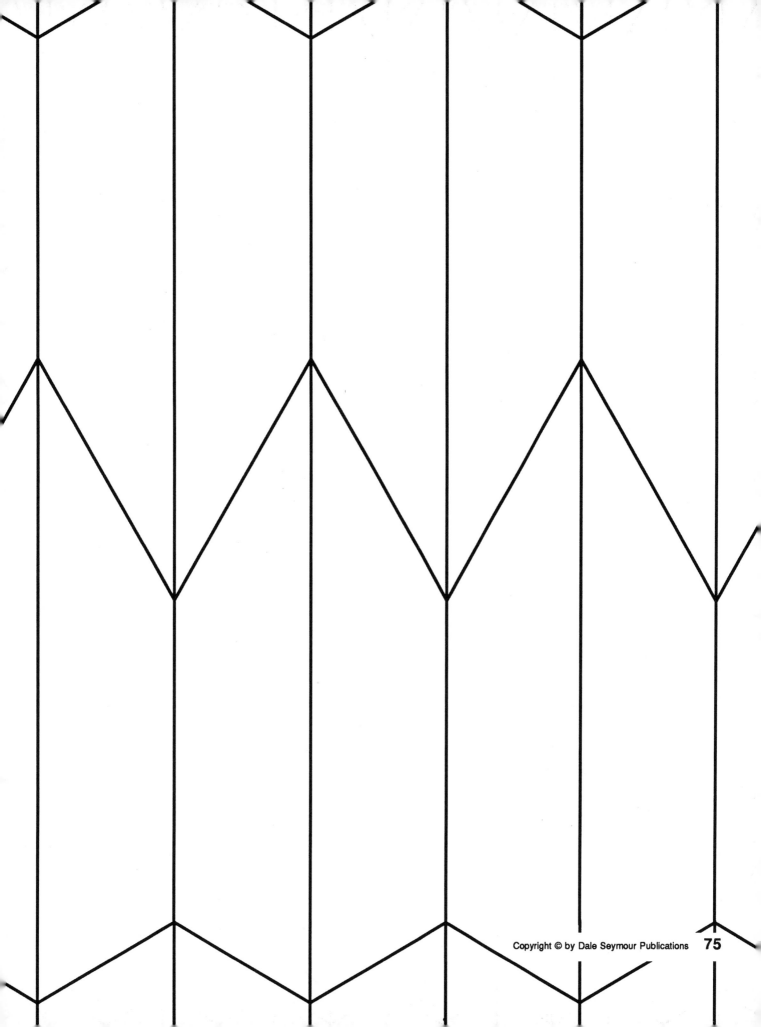

77

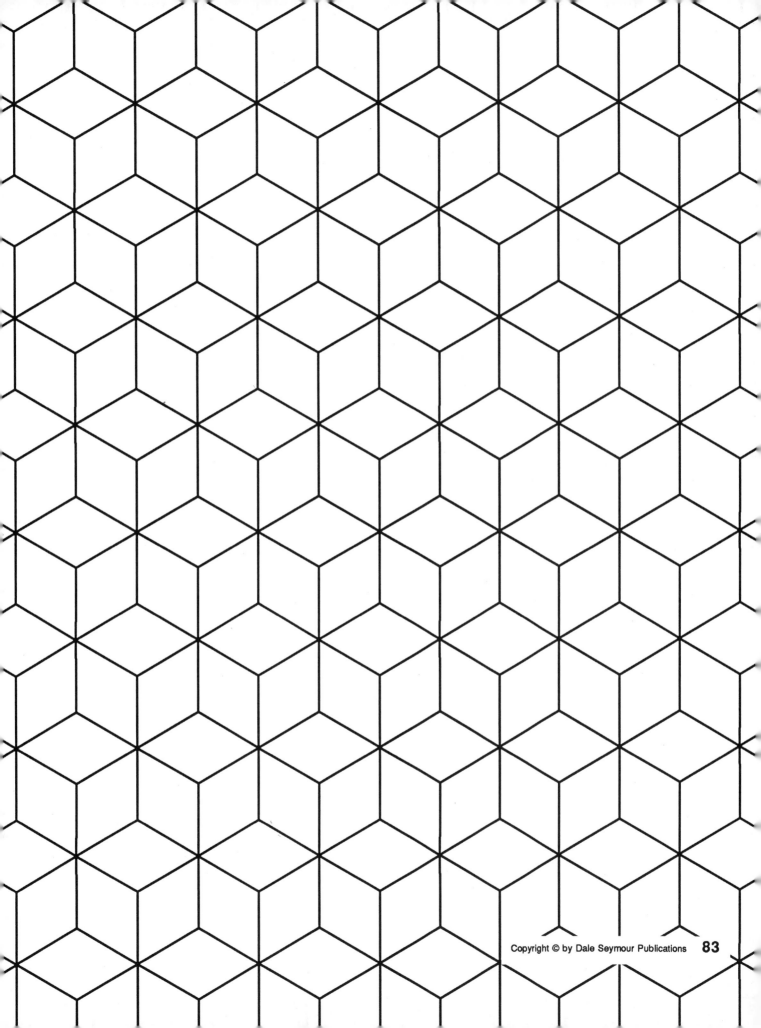

87

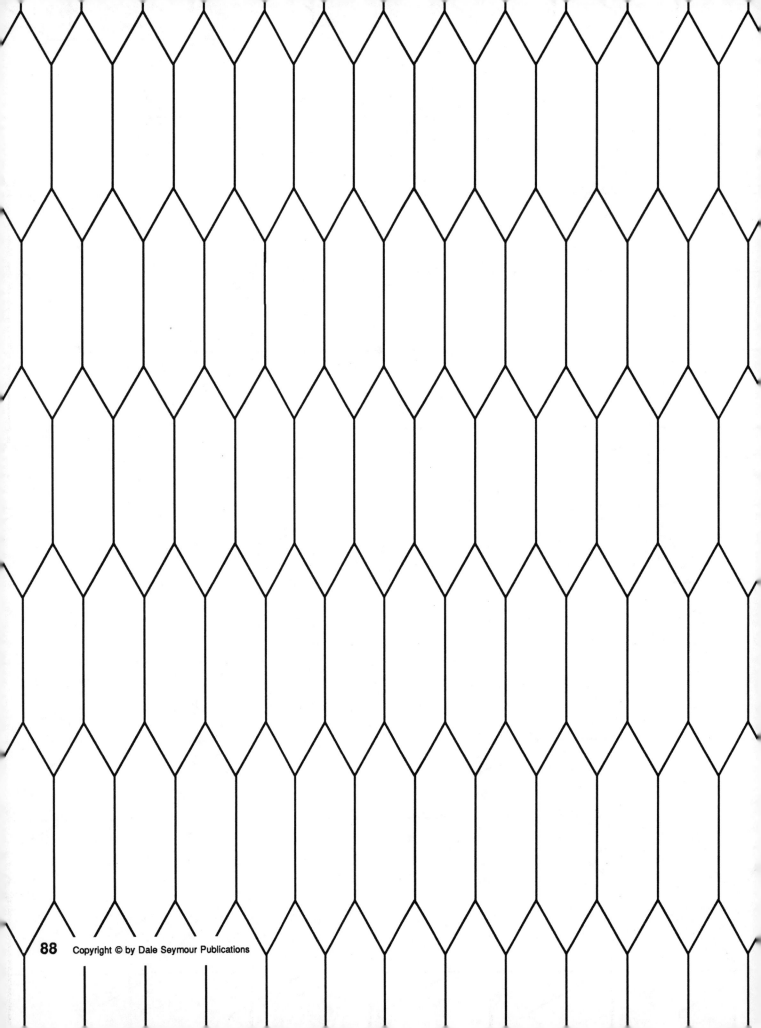

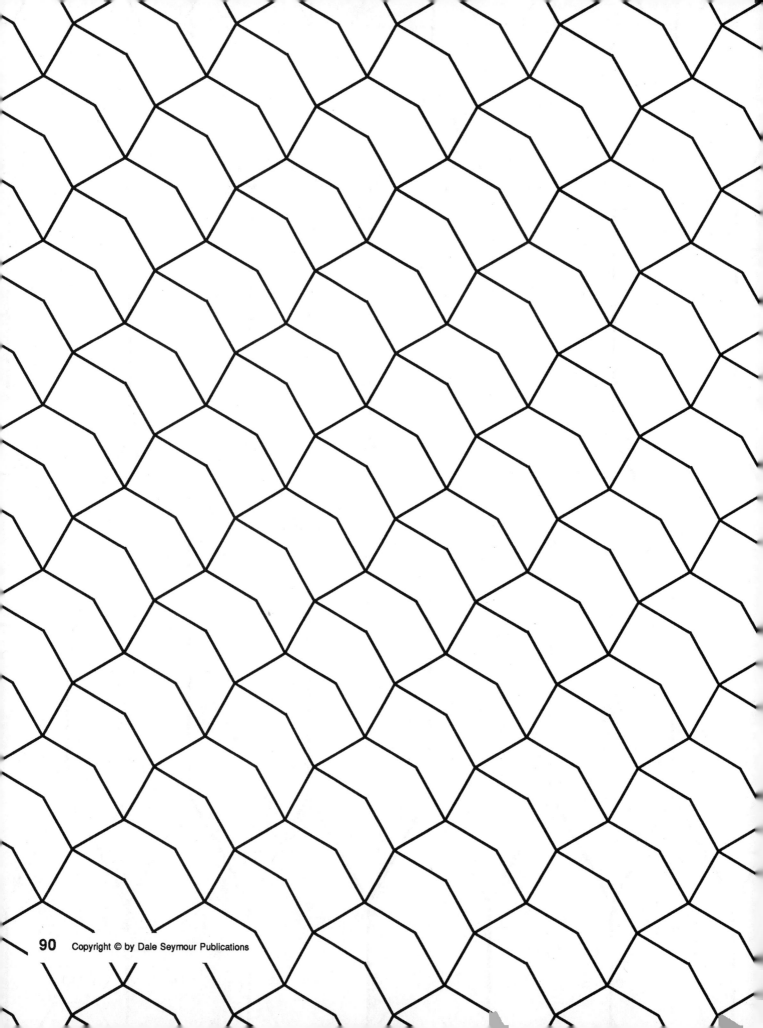

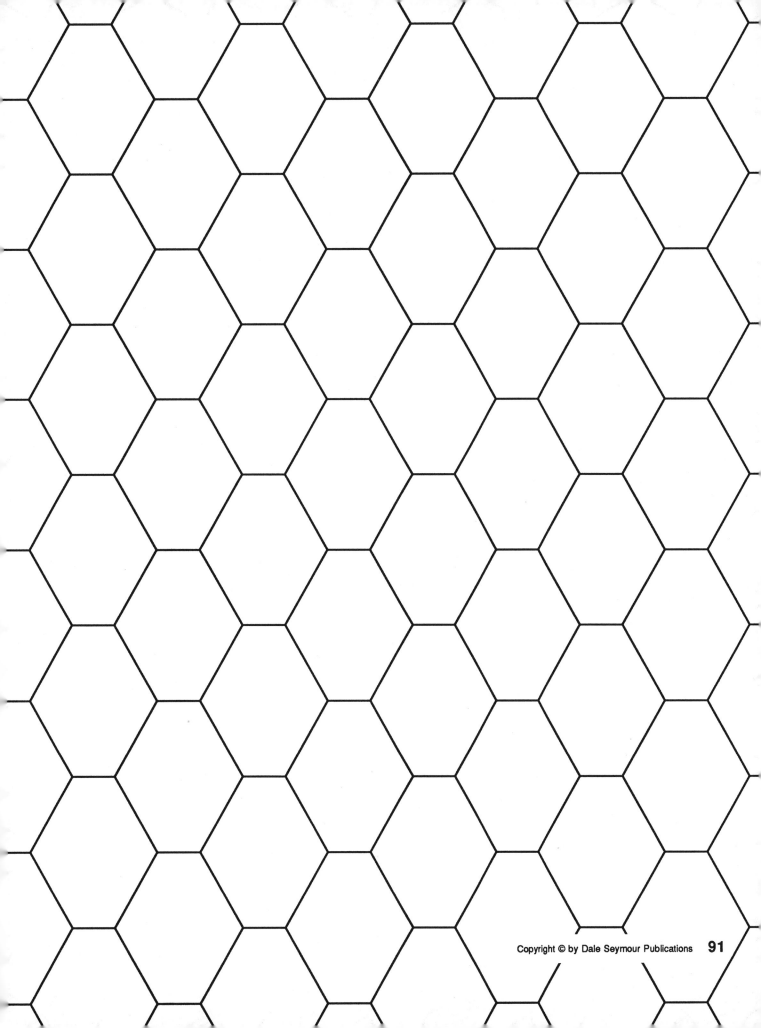

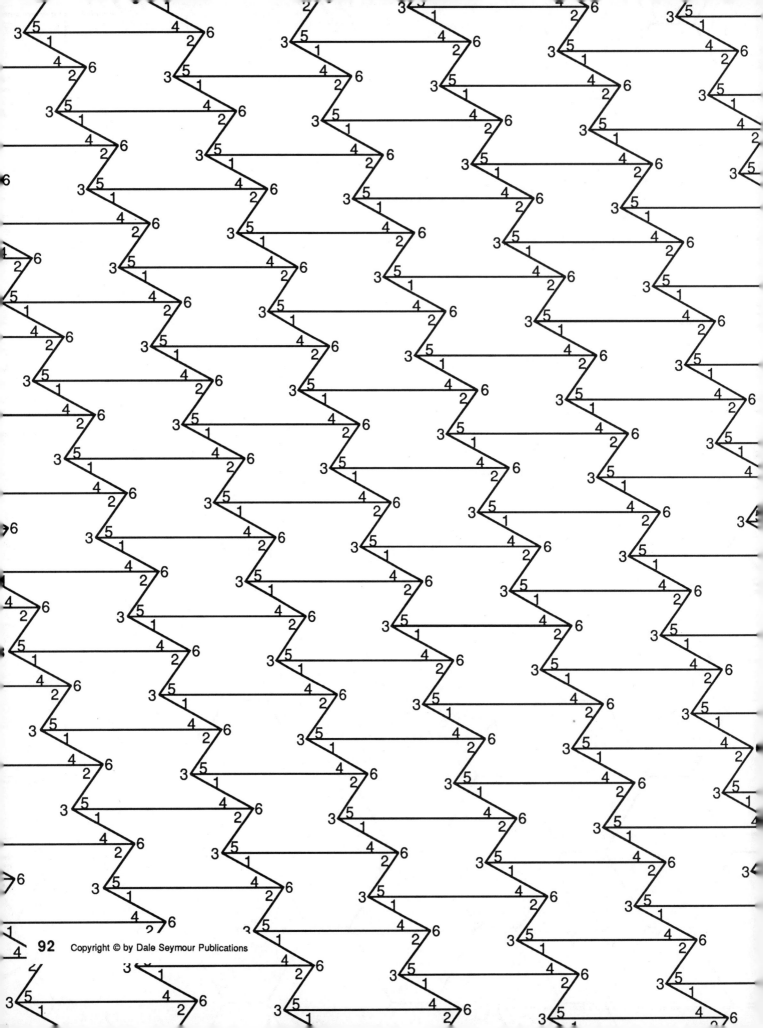

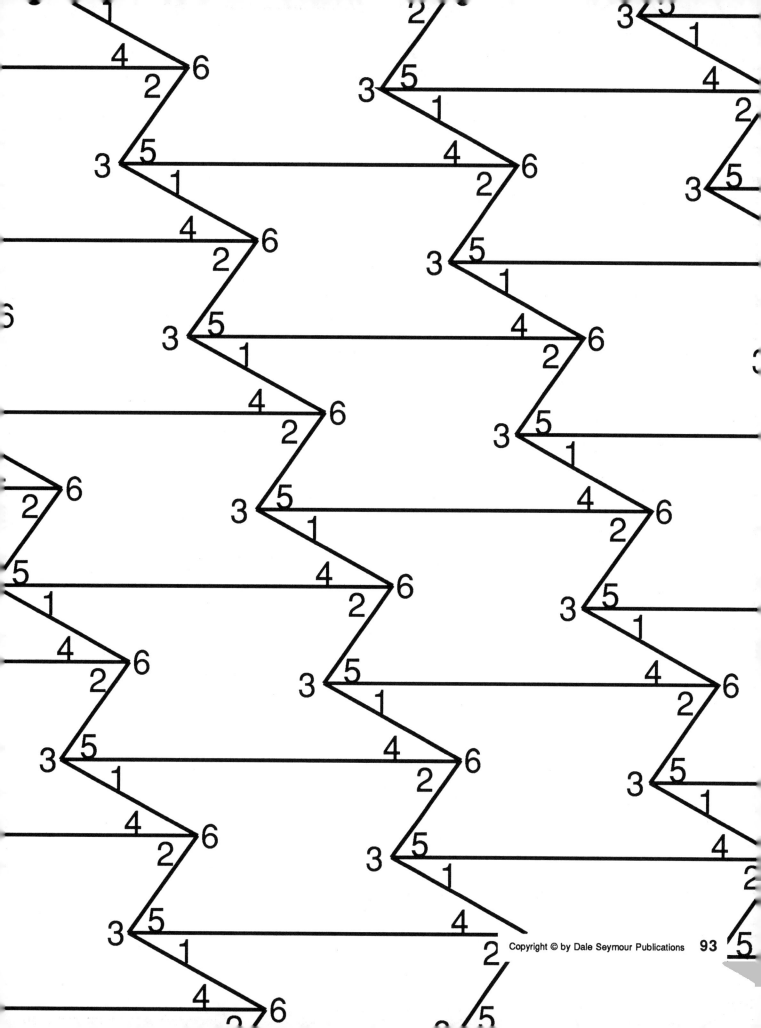

SEMIREGULAR TESSELLATIONS

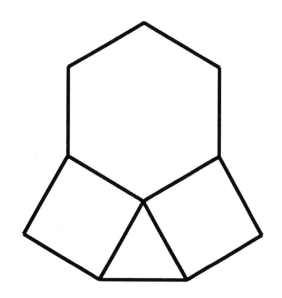

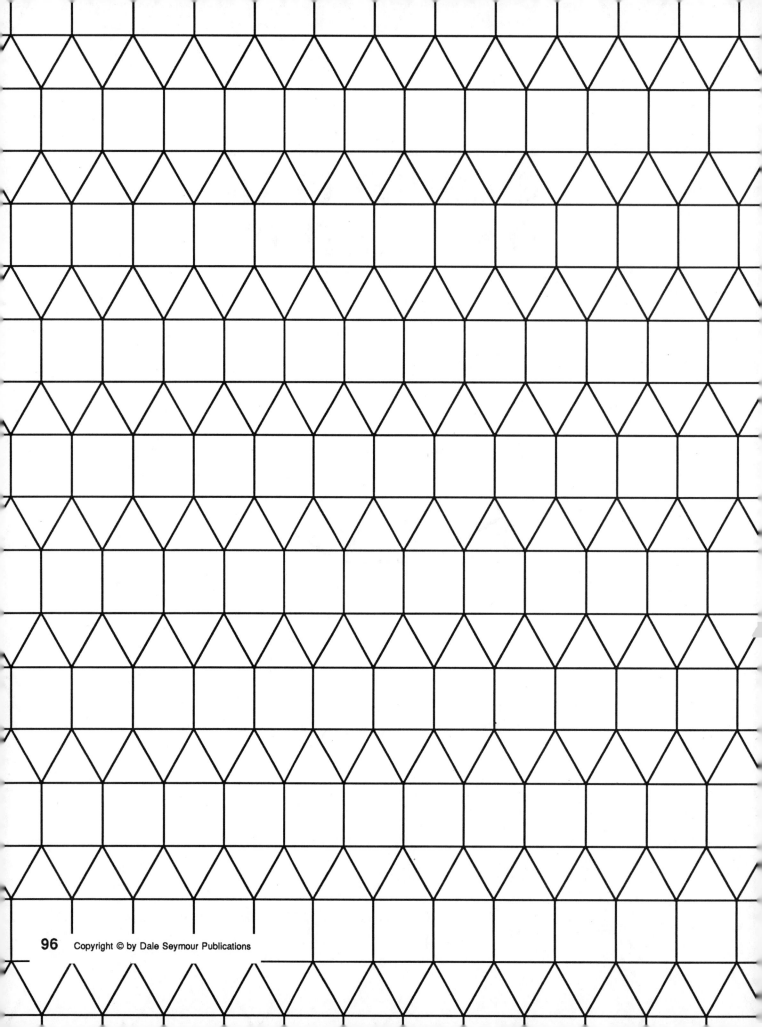

97

99

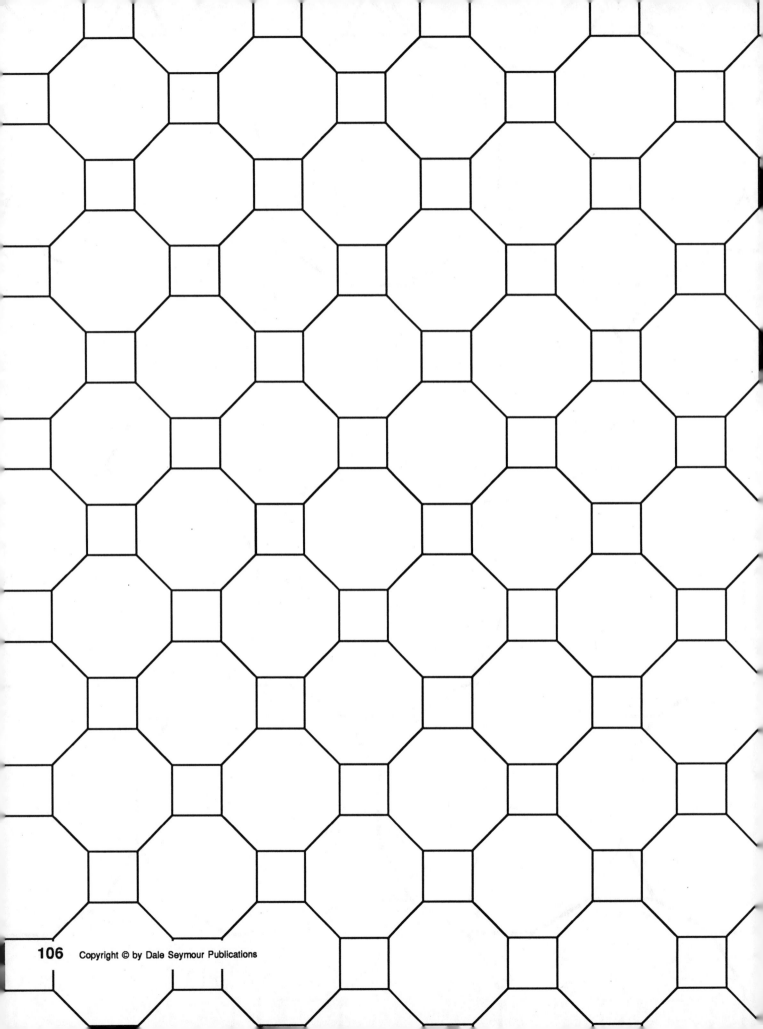

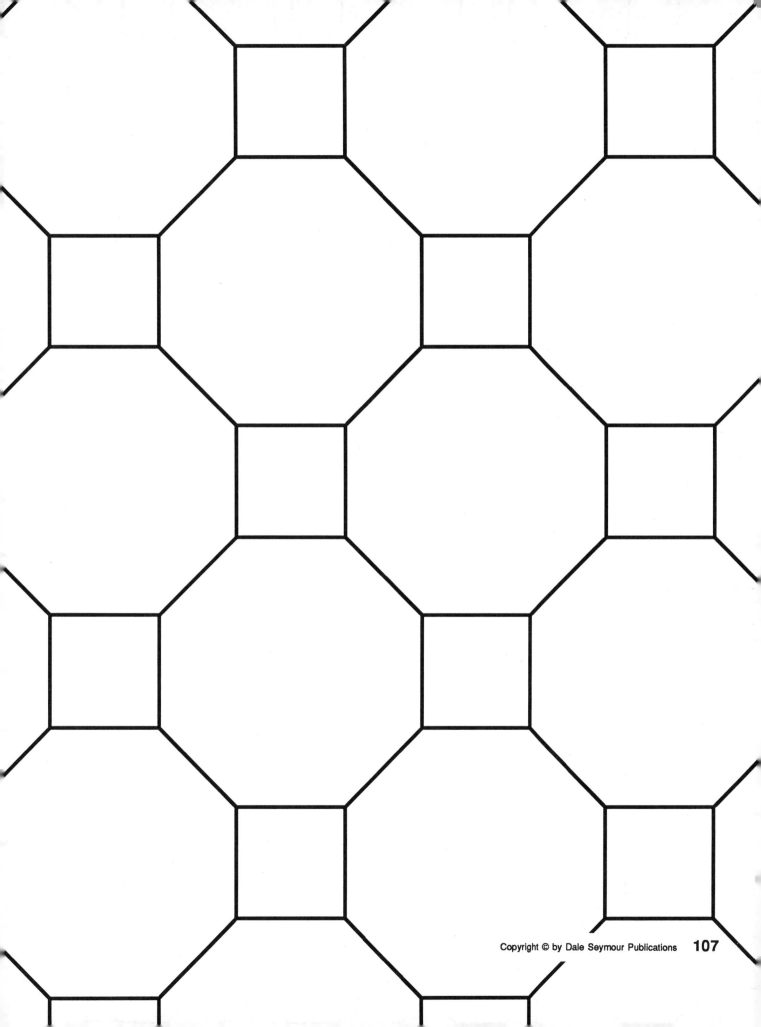

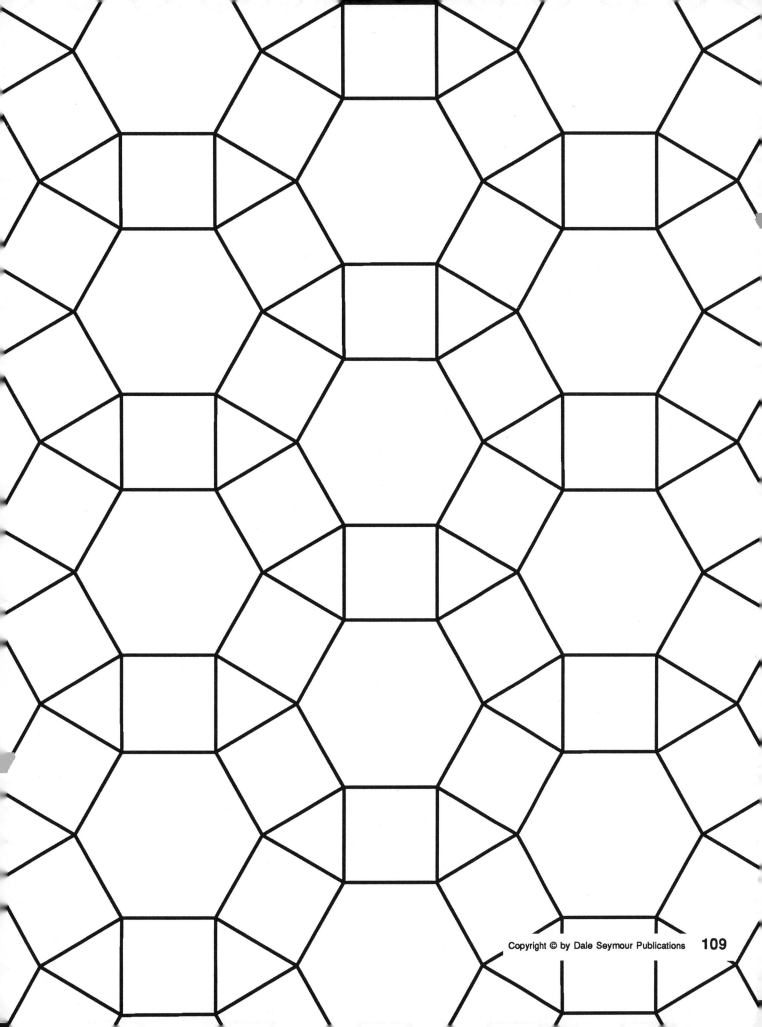

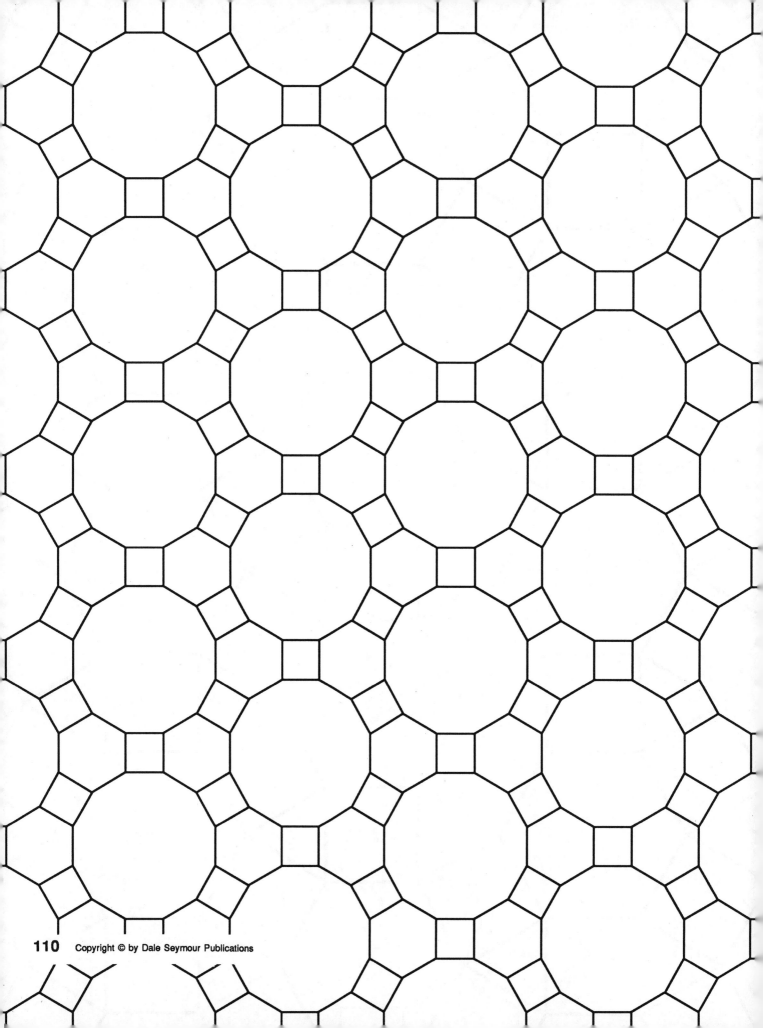

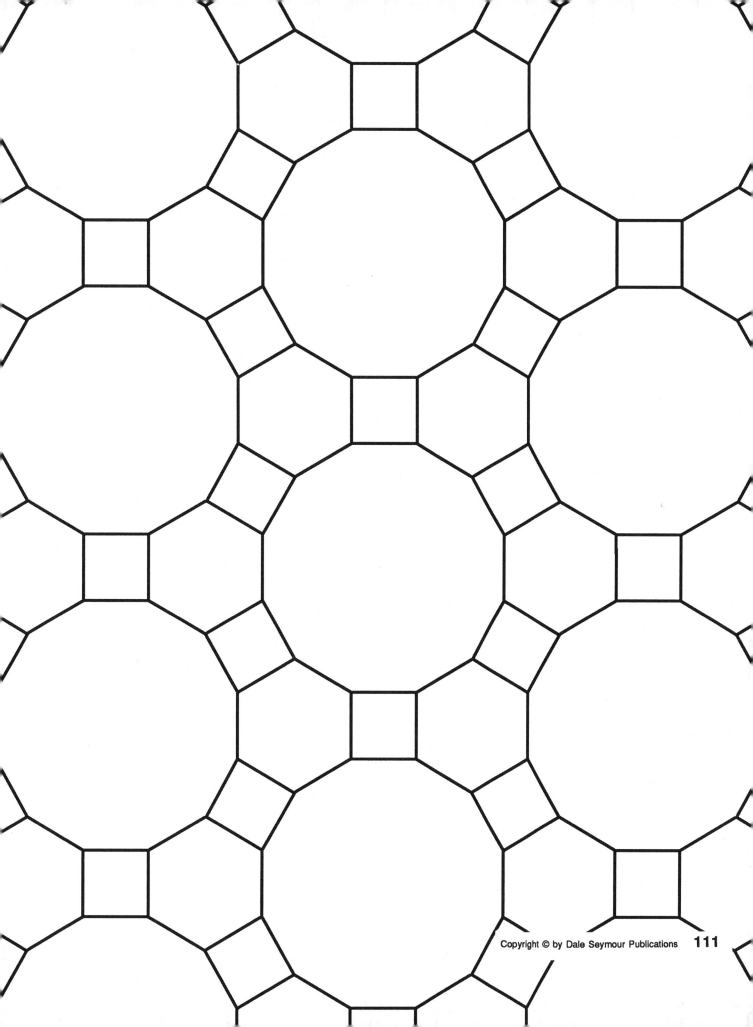

111

SEMIREGULAR TESSELLATIONS

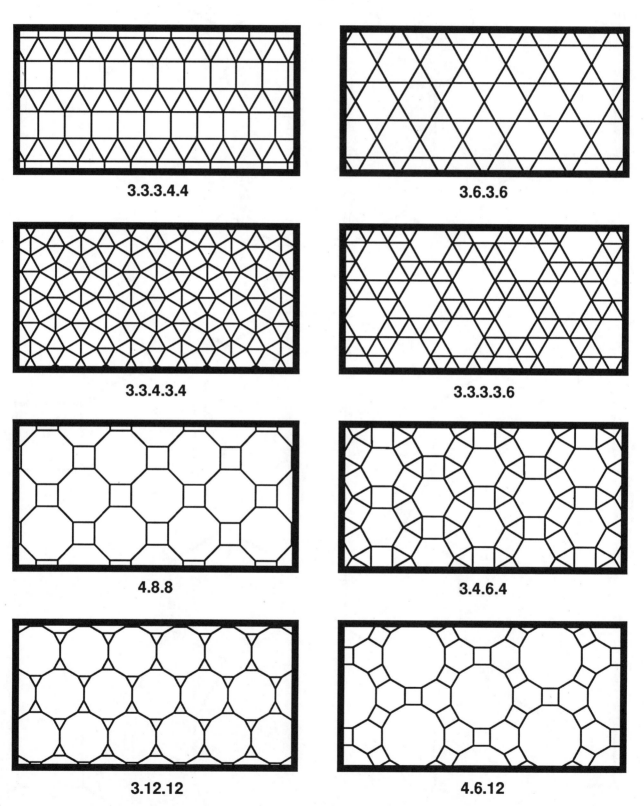

3.3.3.4.4

3.6.3.6

3.3.4.3.4

3.3.3.3.6

4.8.8

3.4.6.4

3.12.12

4.6.12

SAMPLE TESSELLATIONS OF REGULAR POLYGONS WITH TWO OR MORE DIFFERENT VERTICES

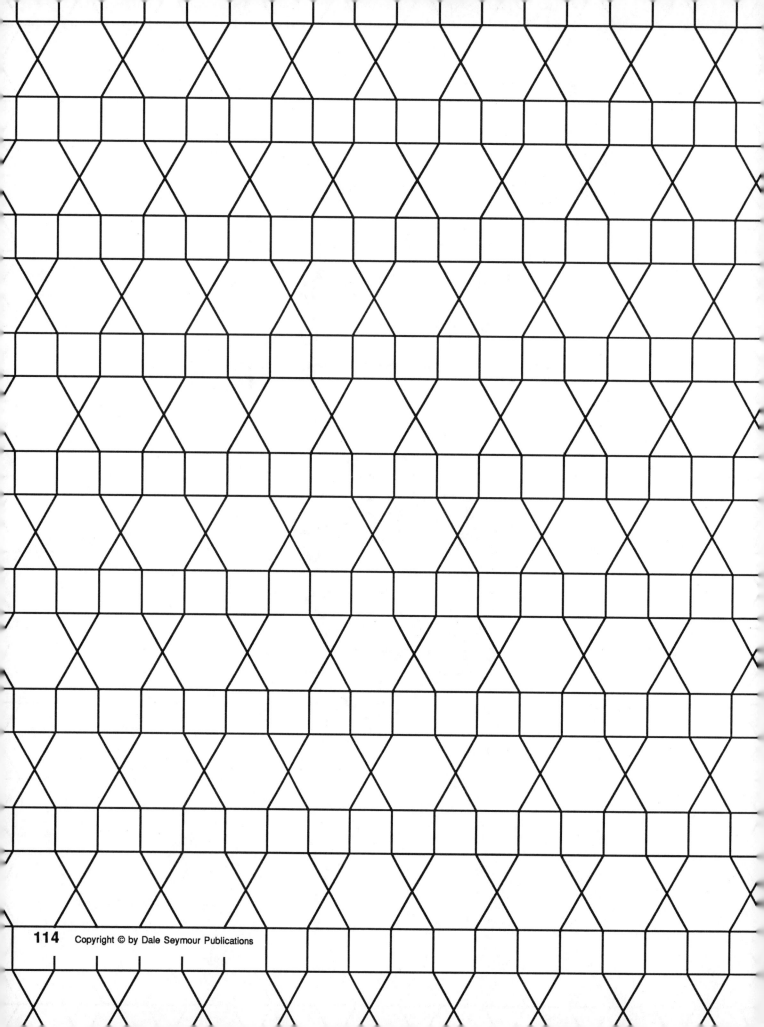

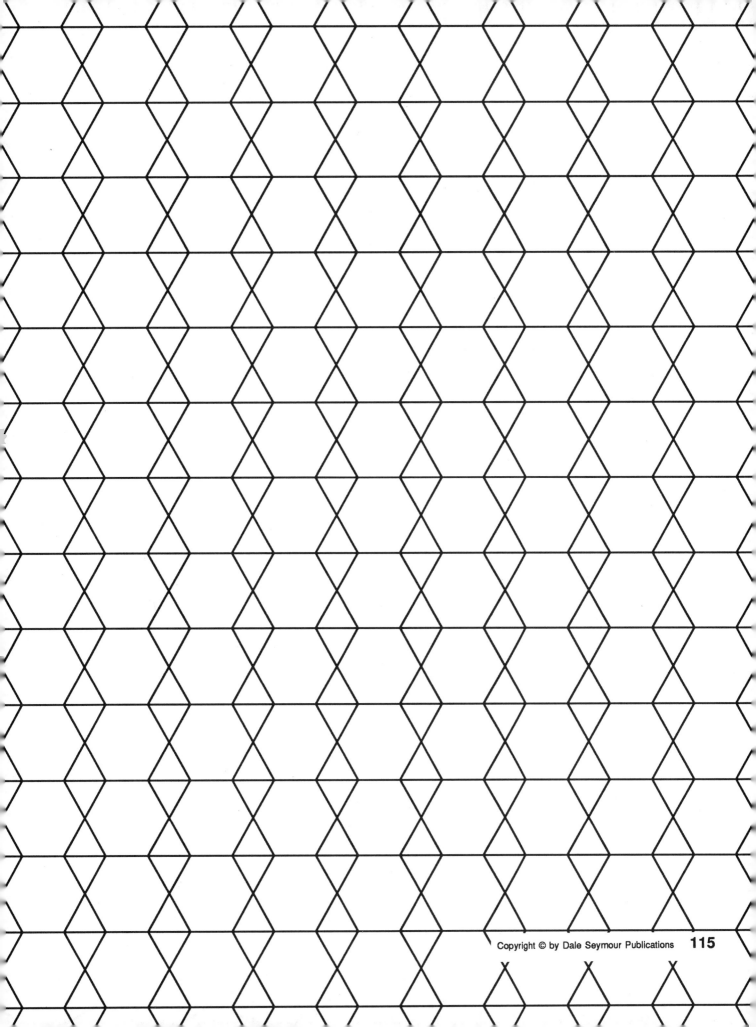

115

117

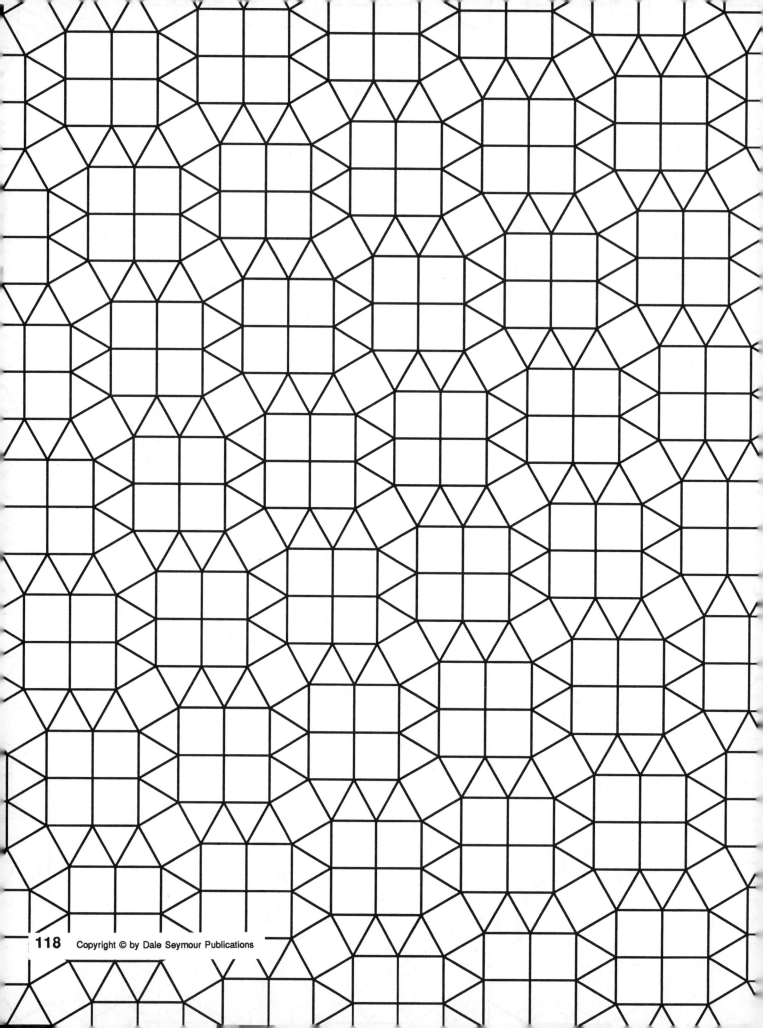

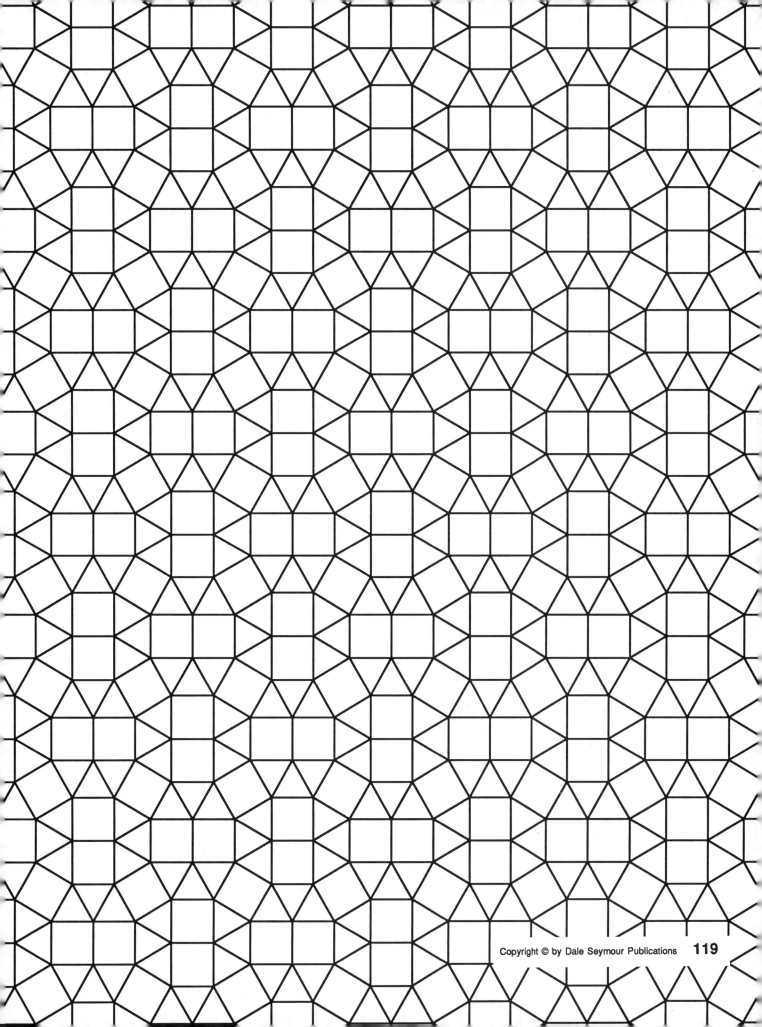

119

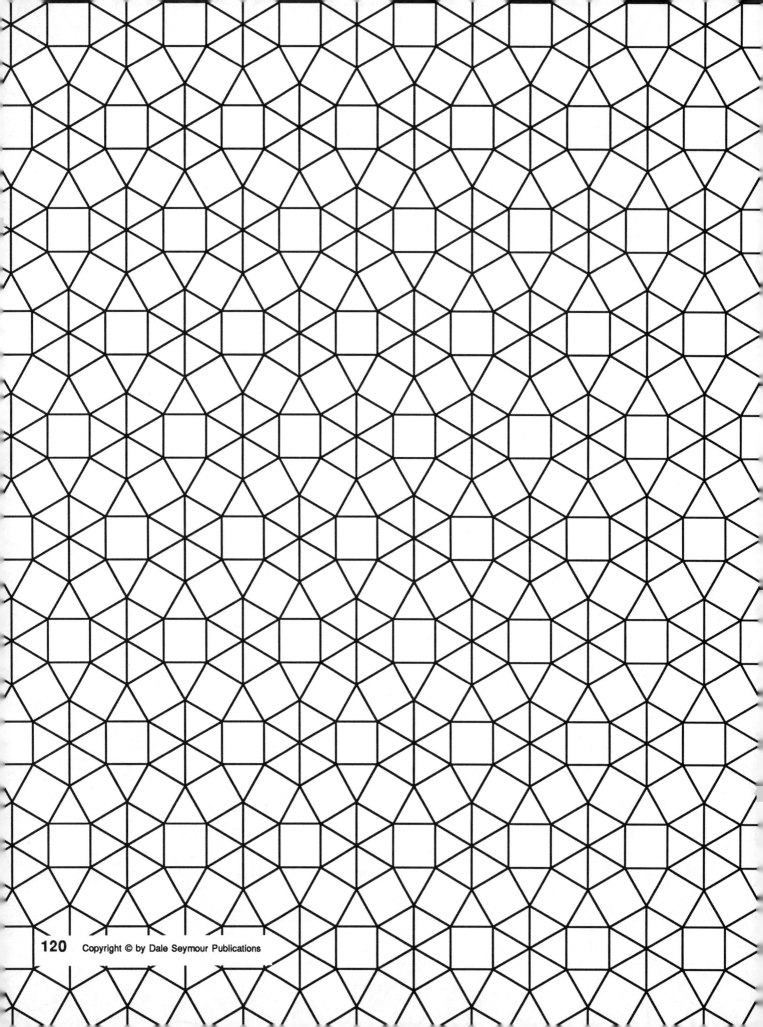

121

123

125

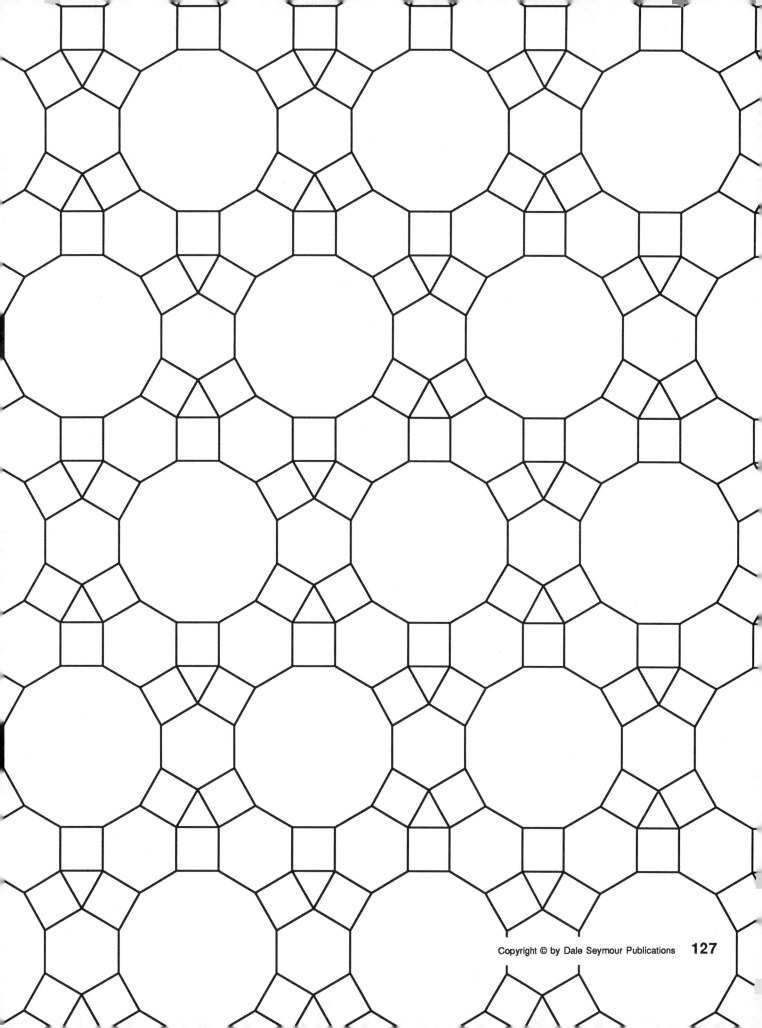

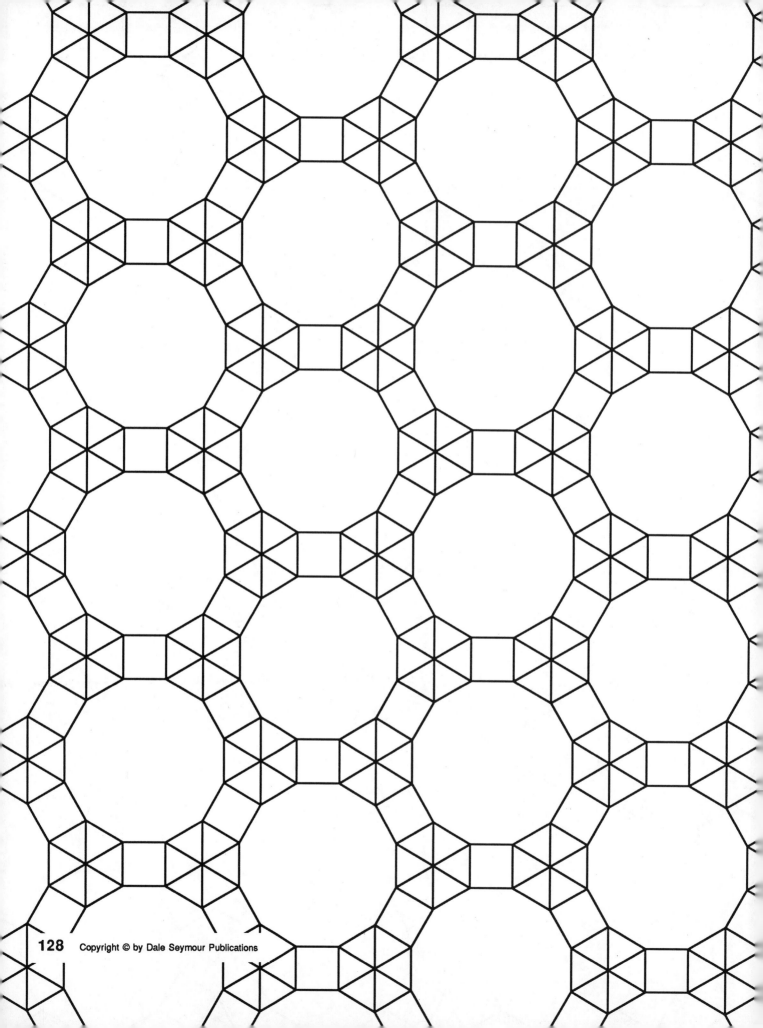

SAMPLE TESSELLATIONS OF STAR POLYGONS

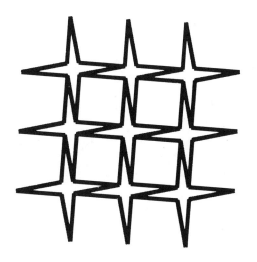

131

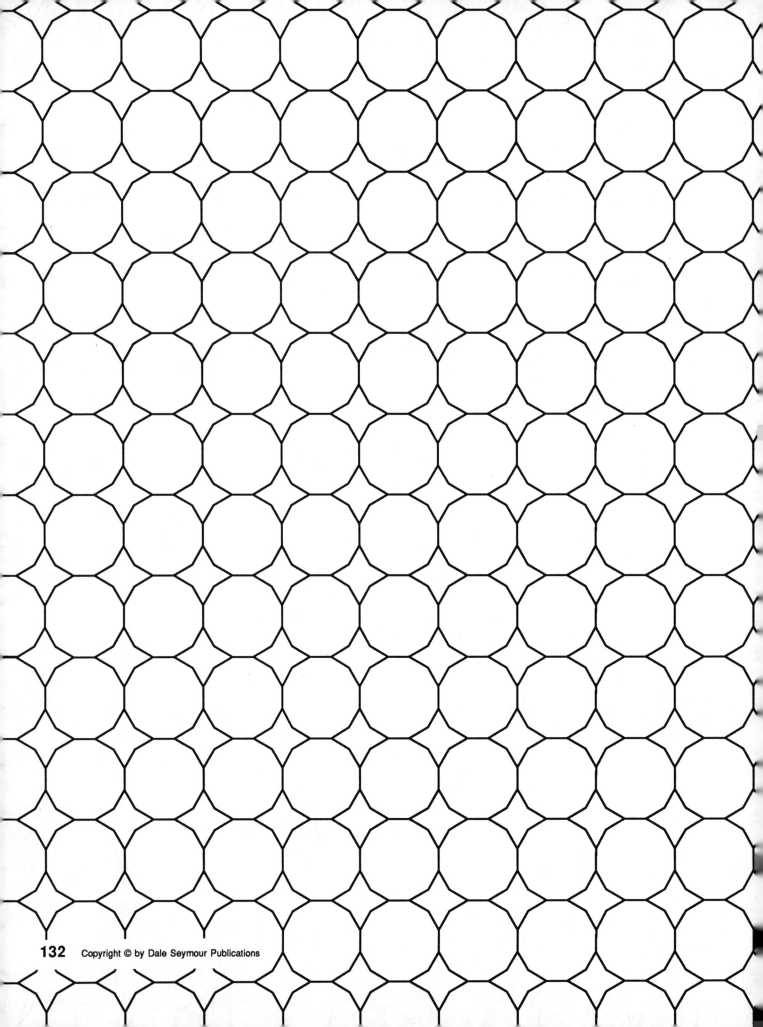

133

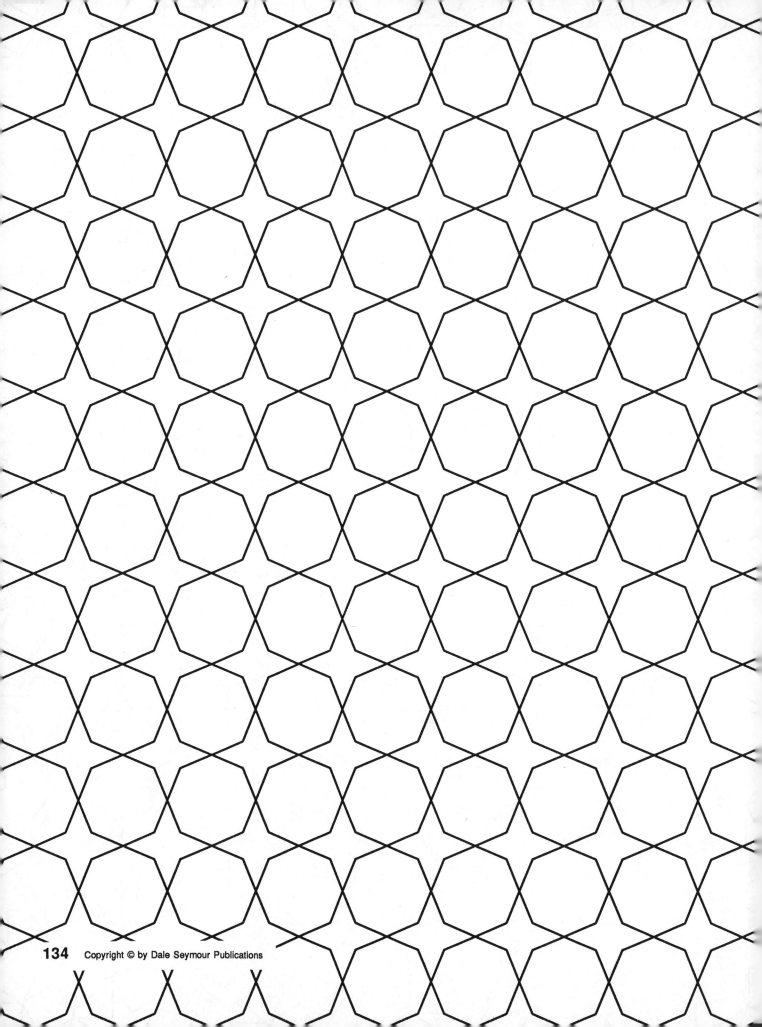

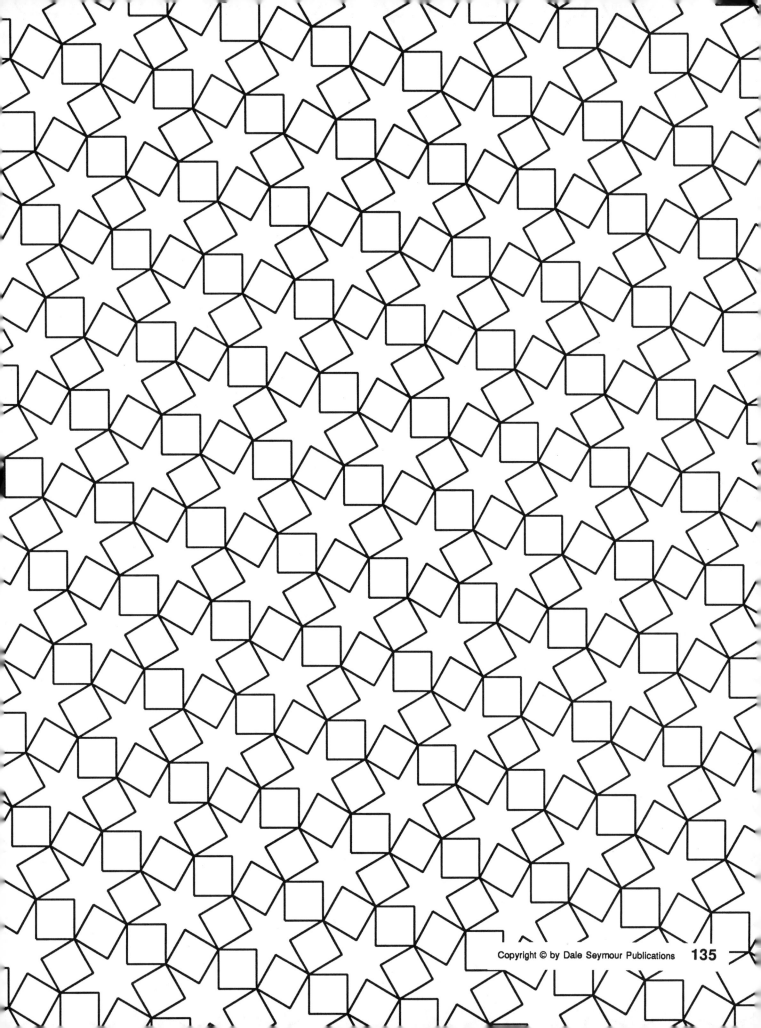

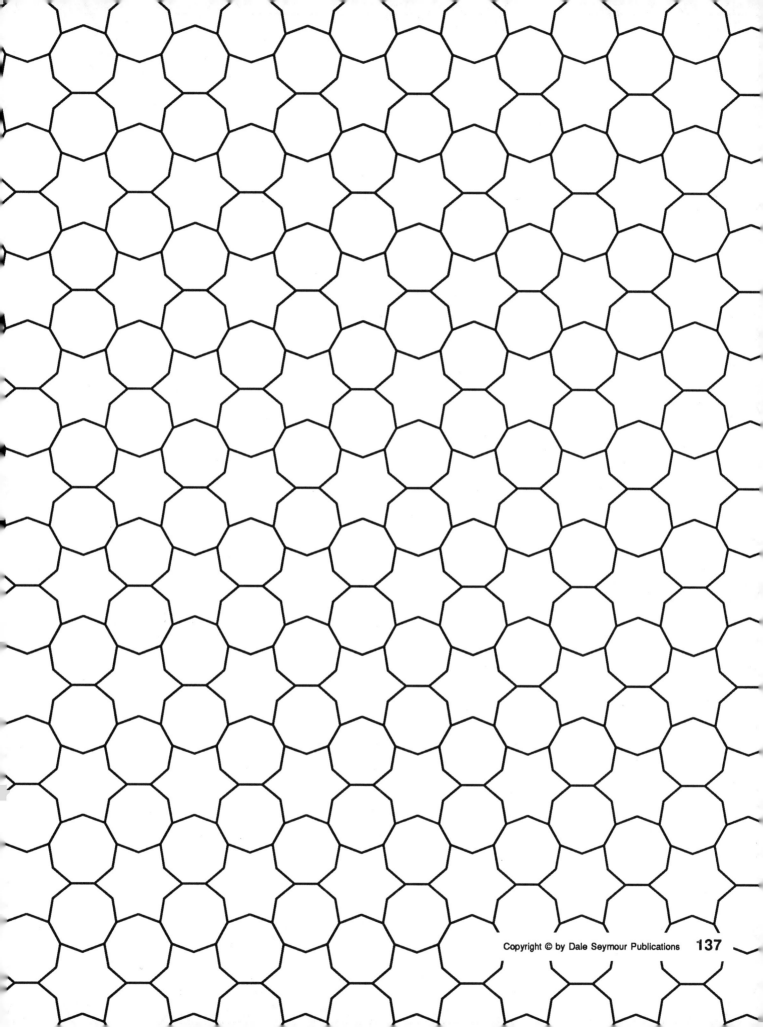

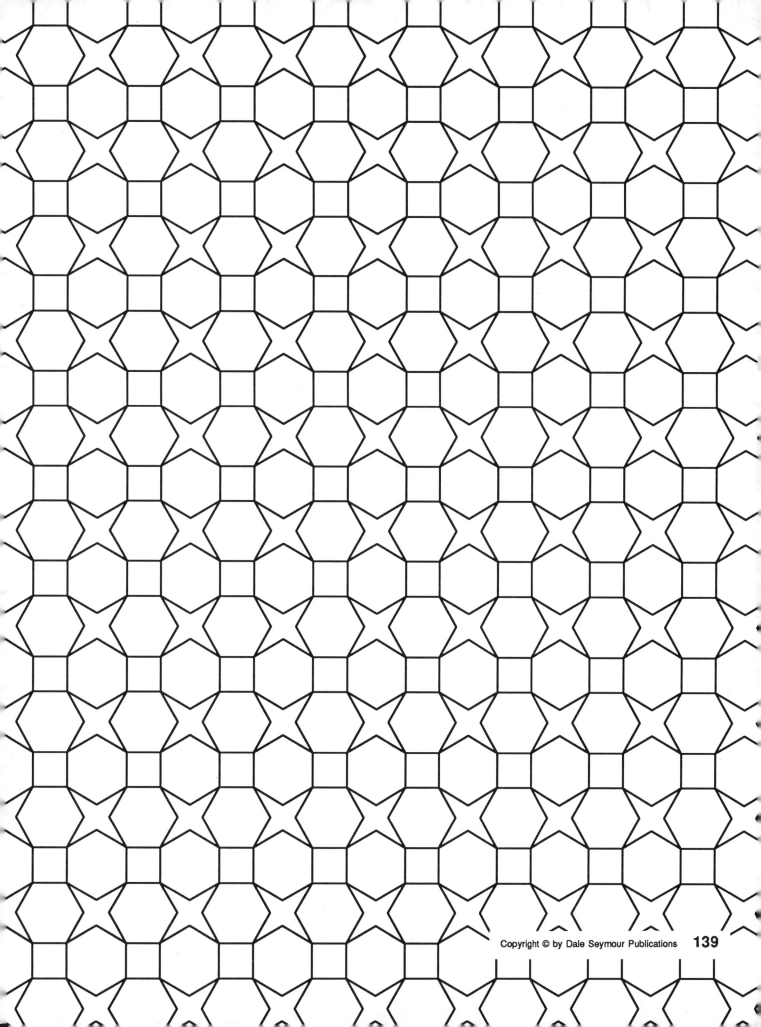

139

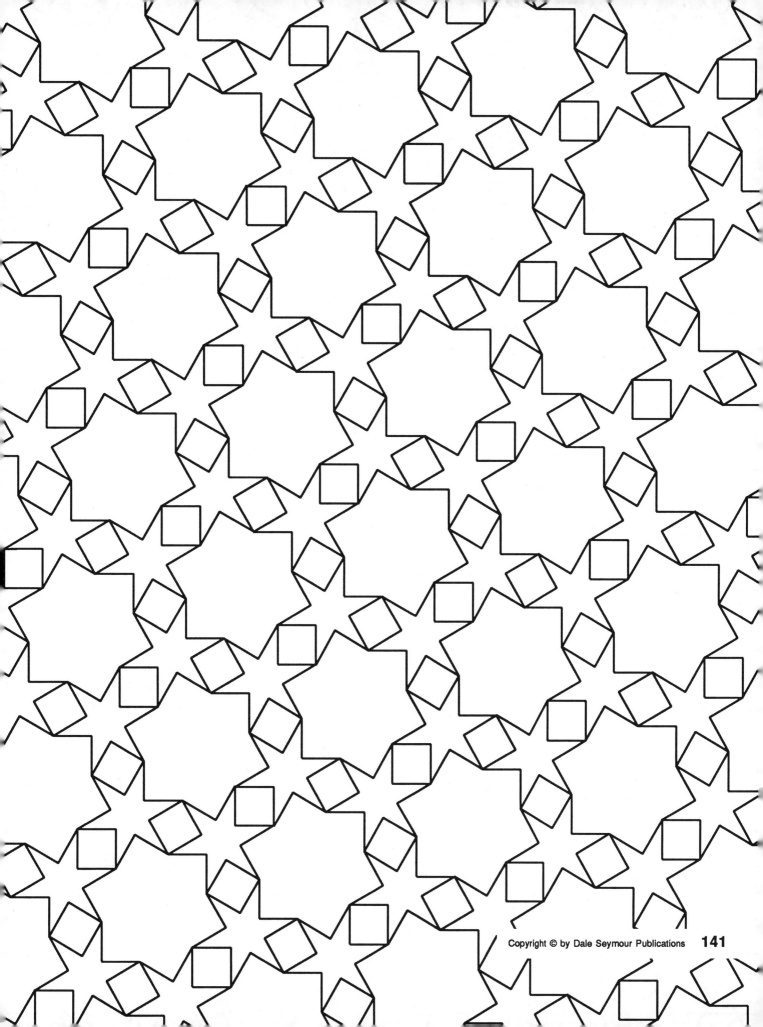

141

143

144 Copyright © by Dale Seymour Publications

145

SAMPLE TESSELLATIONS OF SINGLE POLYGONAL SHAPES

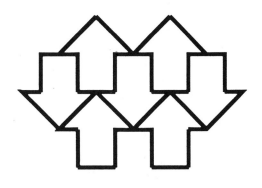

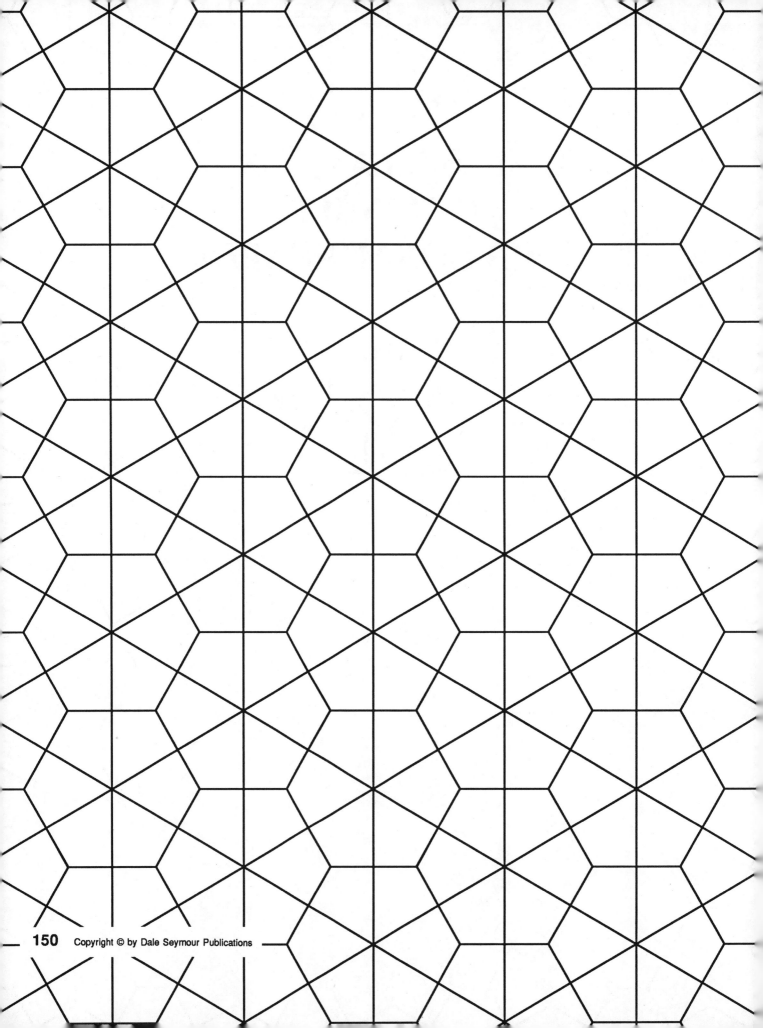

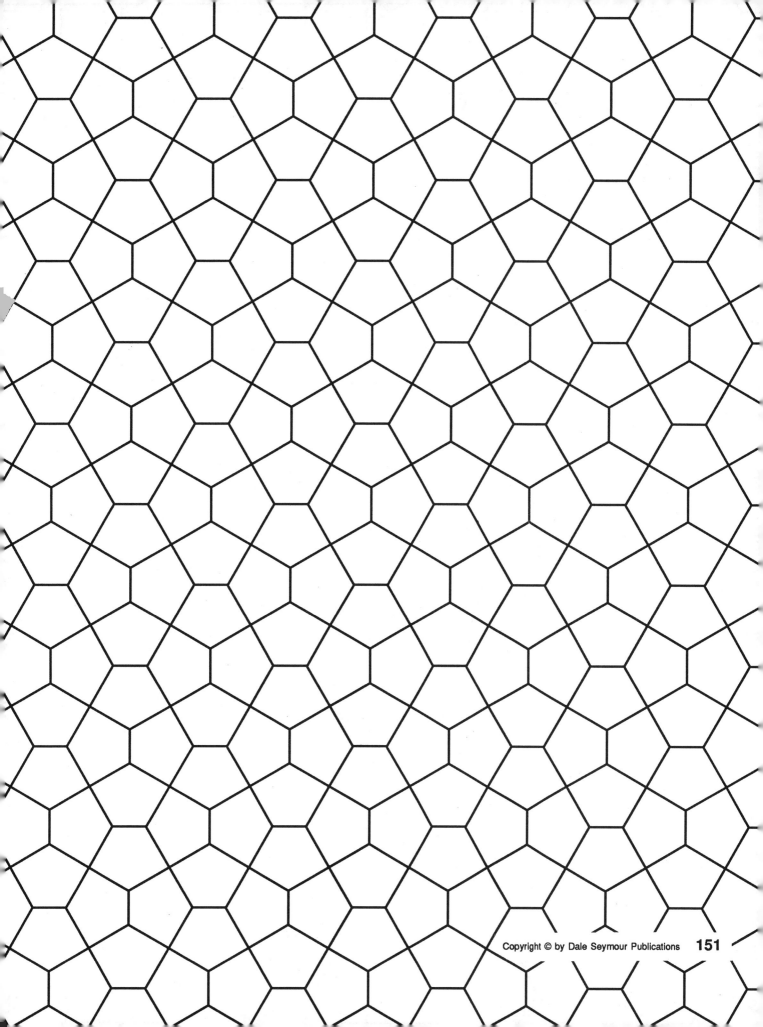

151

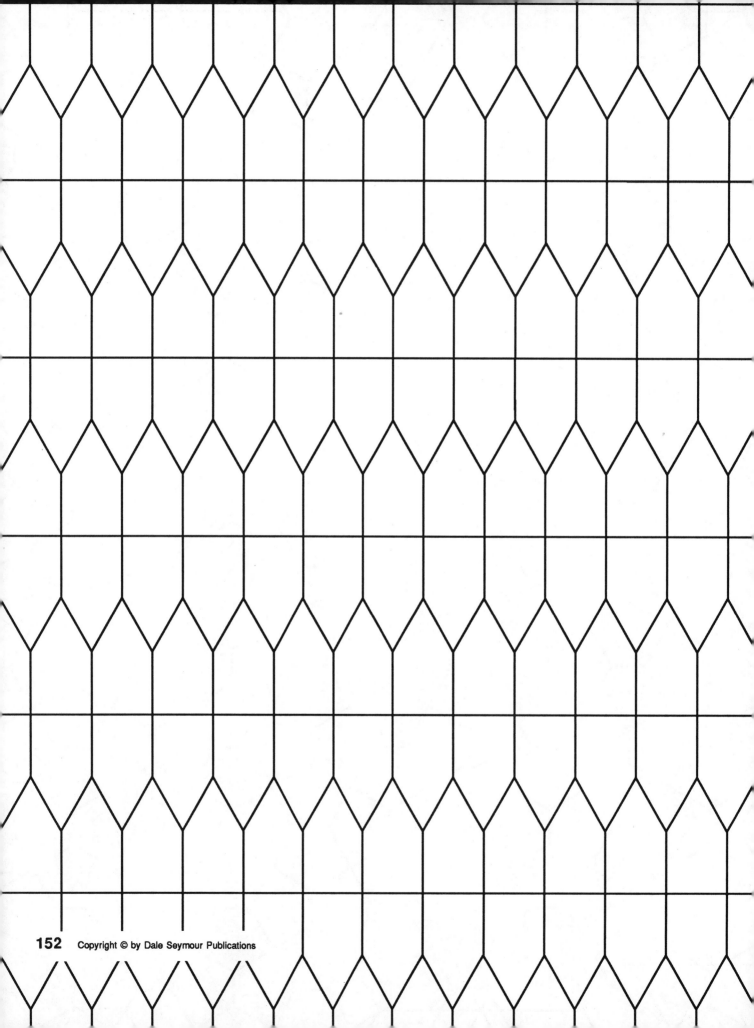

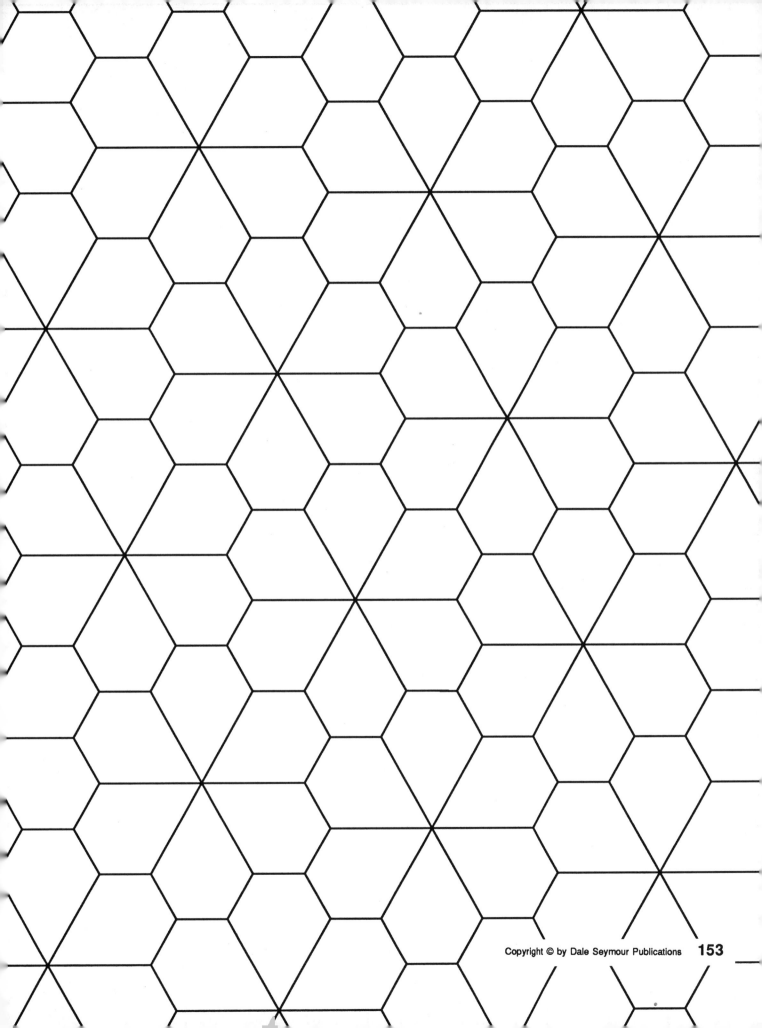

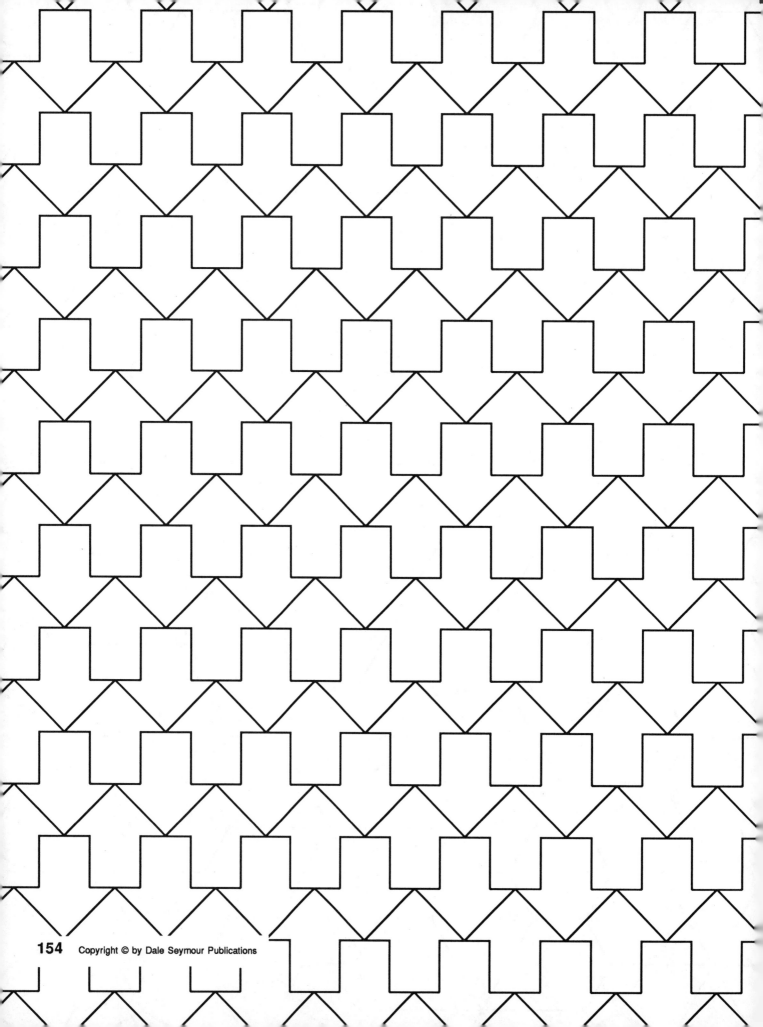

155

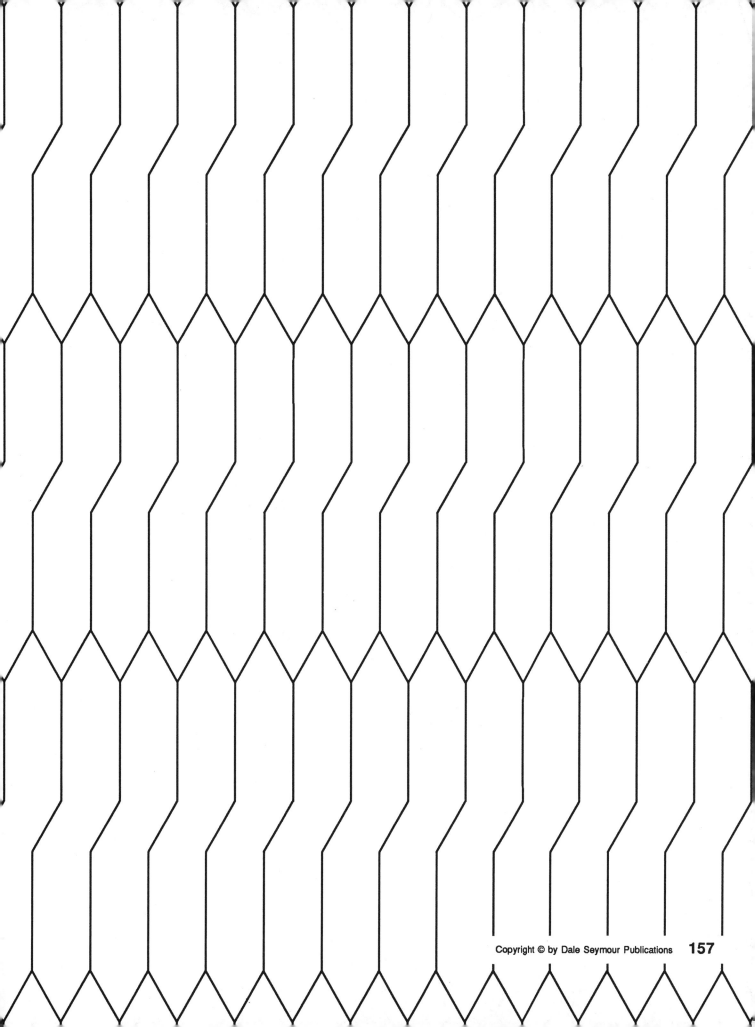

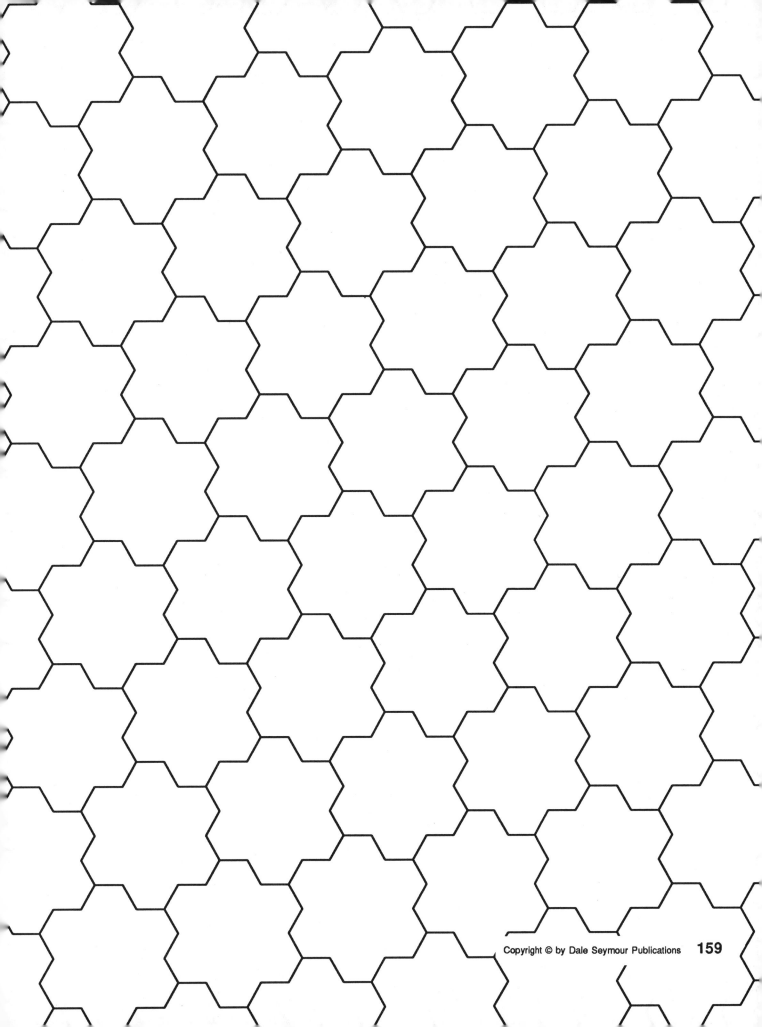

159

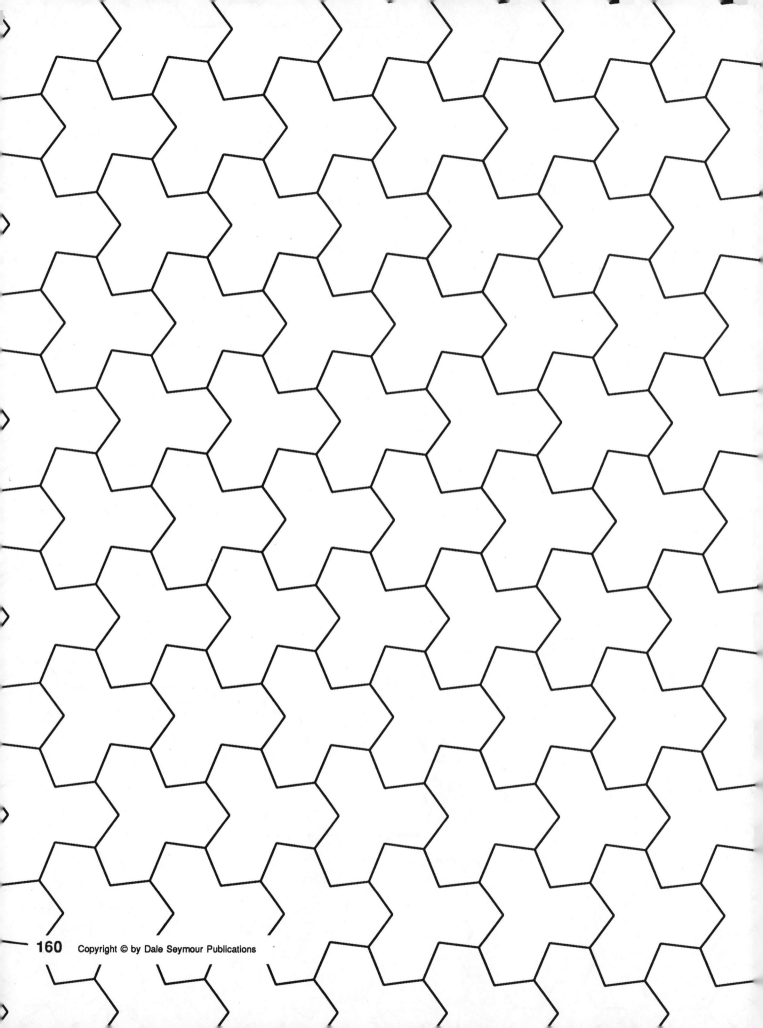

161

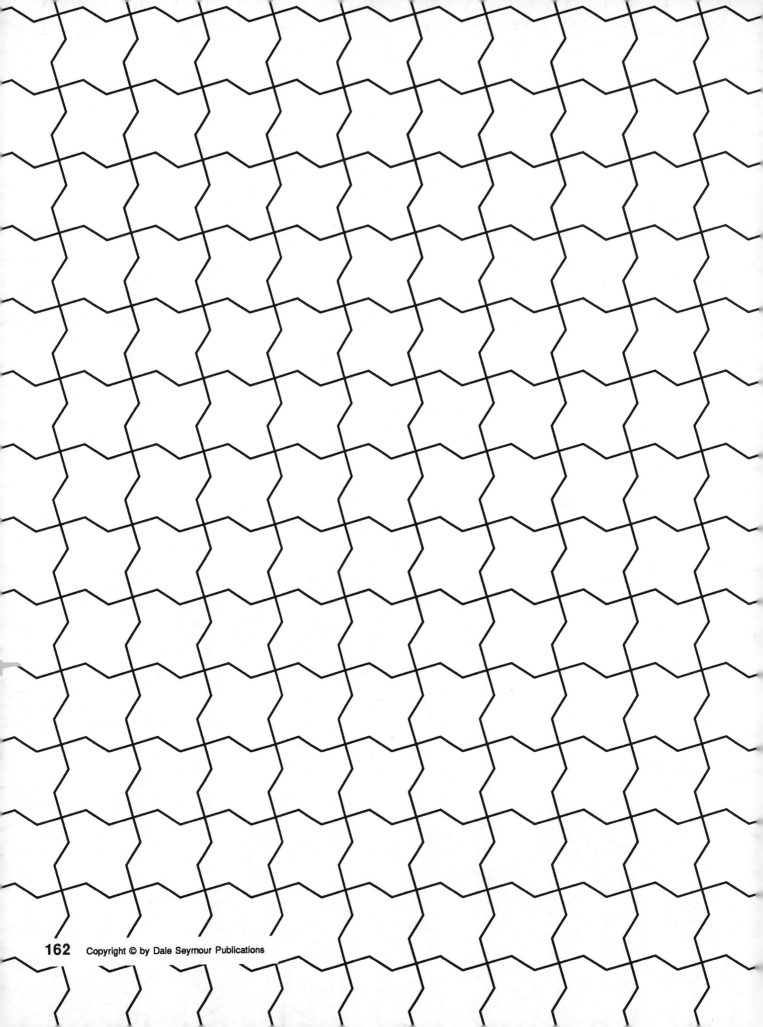

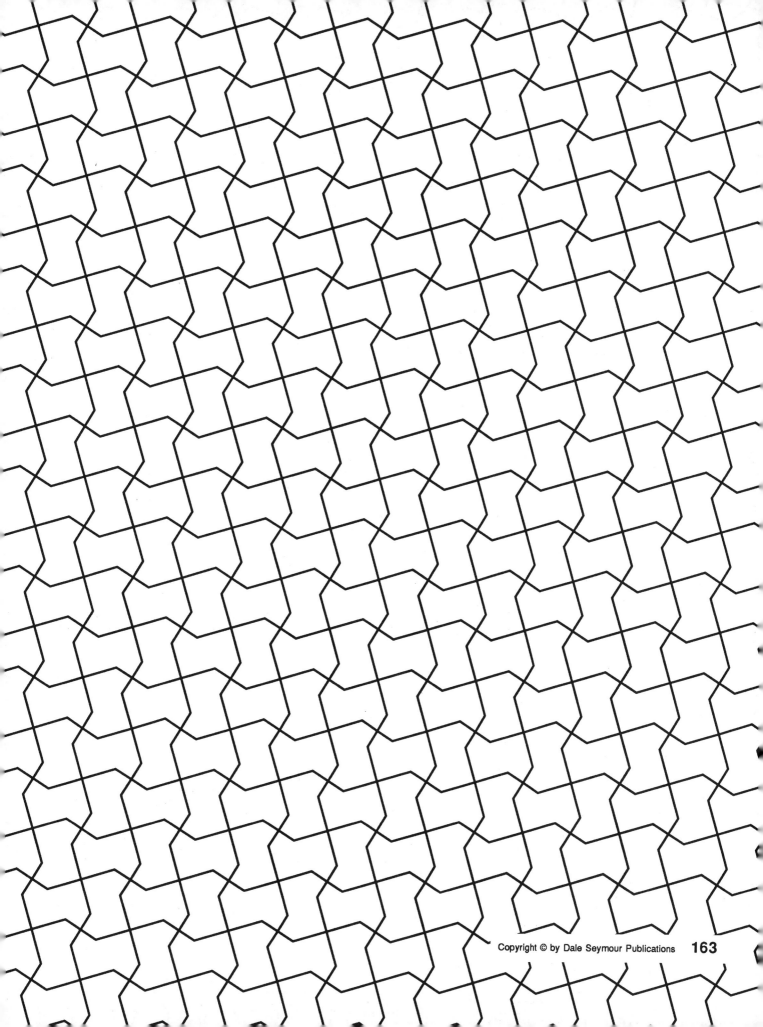

163

165

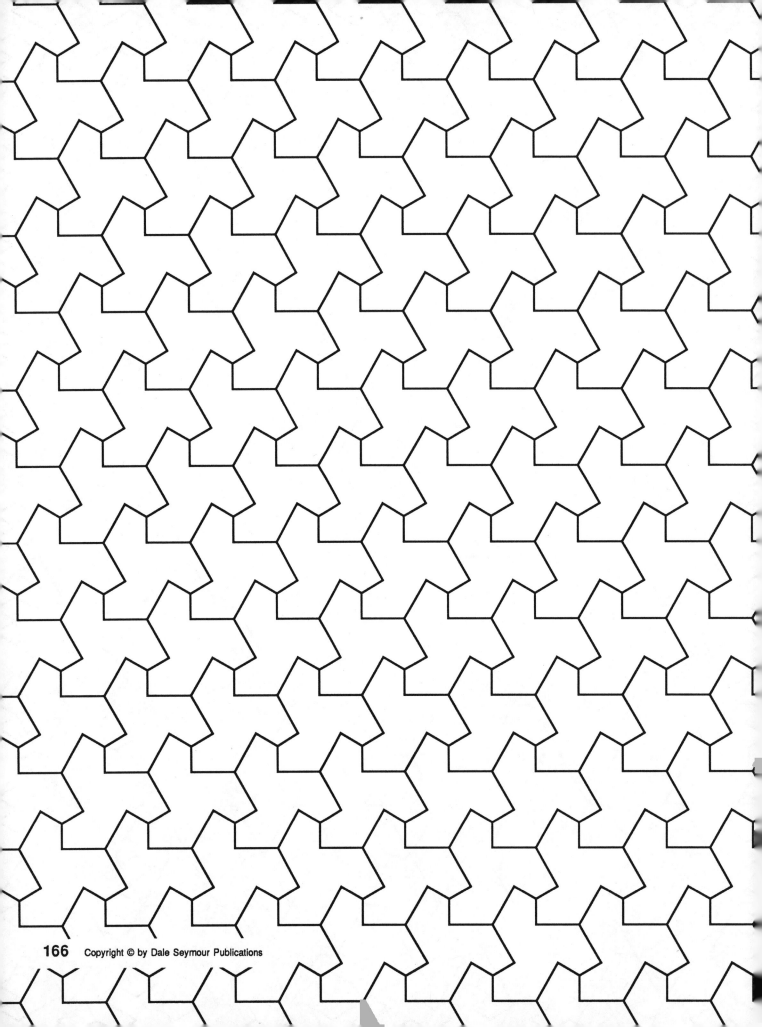

166

167

169

SAMPLE TESSELLATIONS OF MULTIPLE POLYGONAL SHAPES

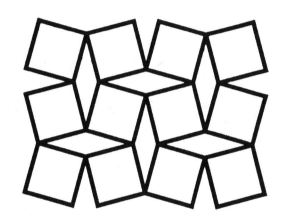

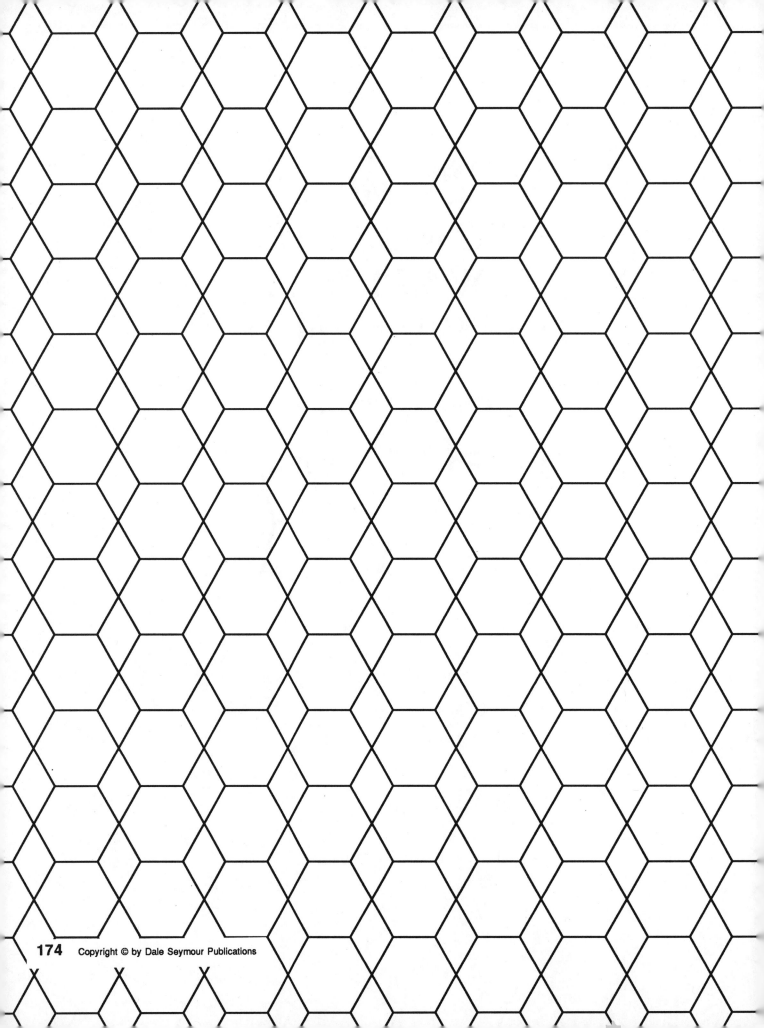

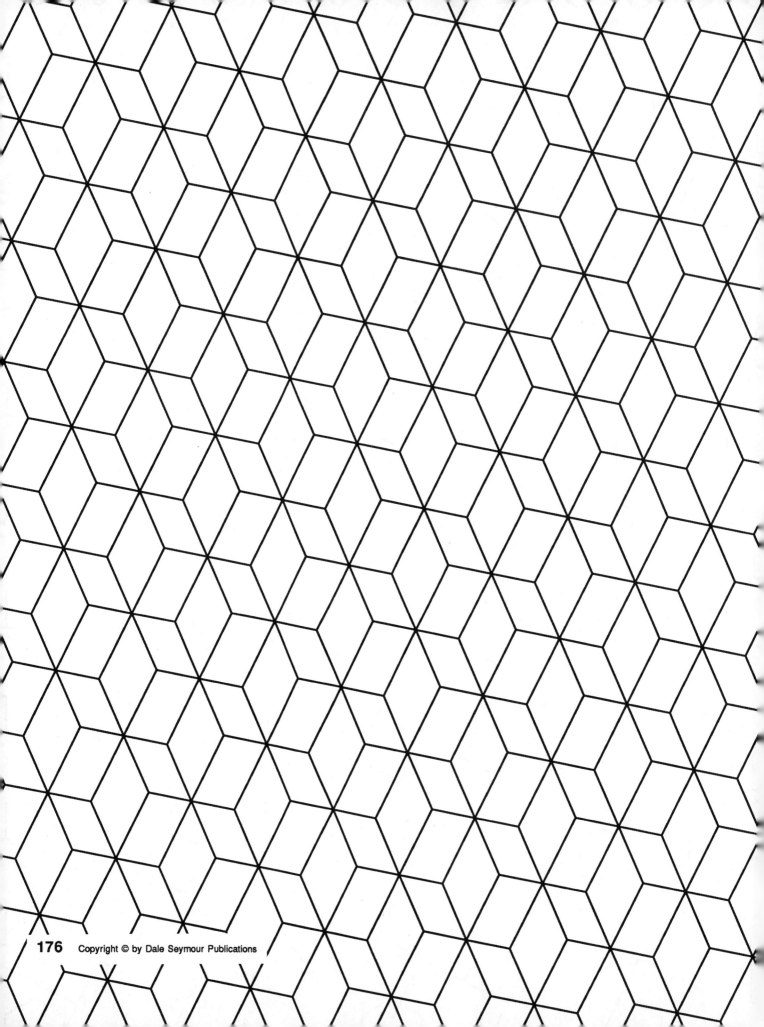

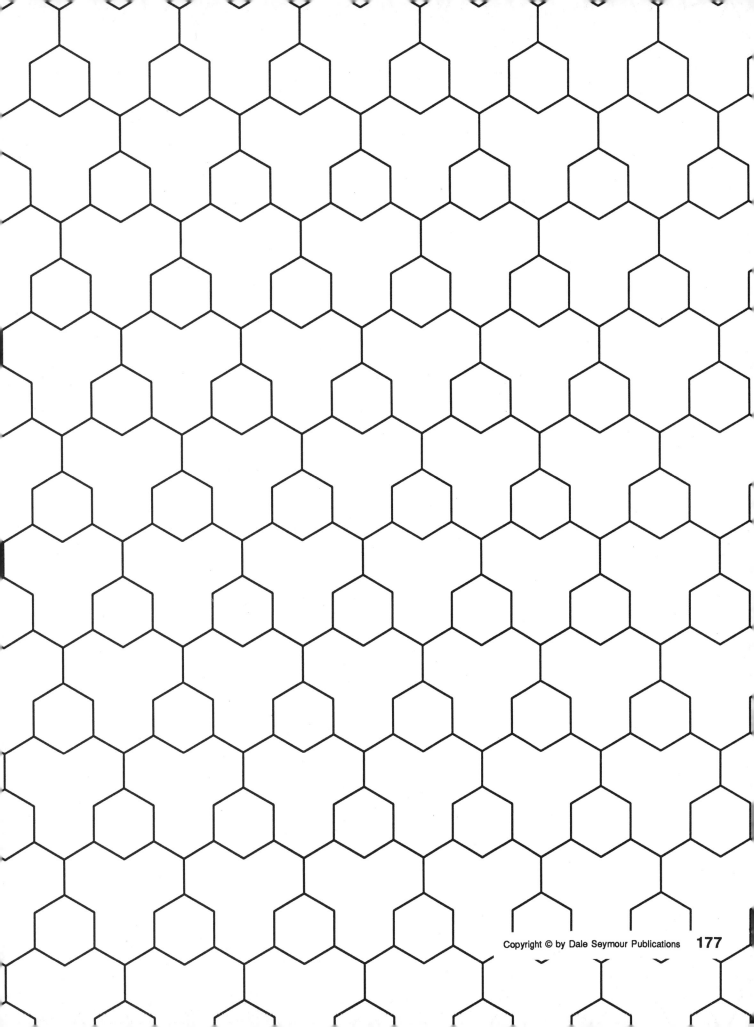

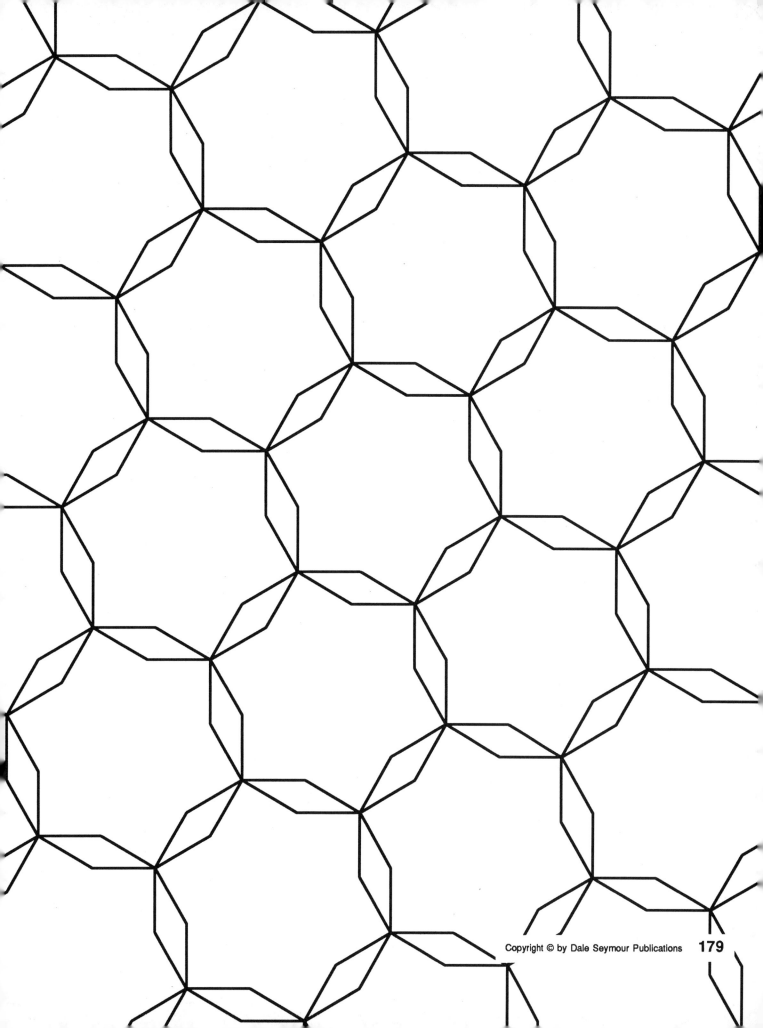

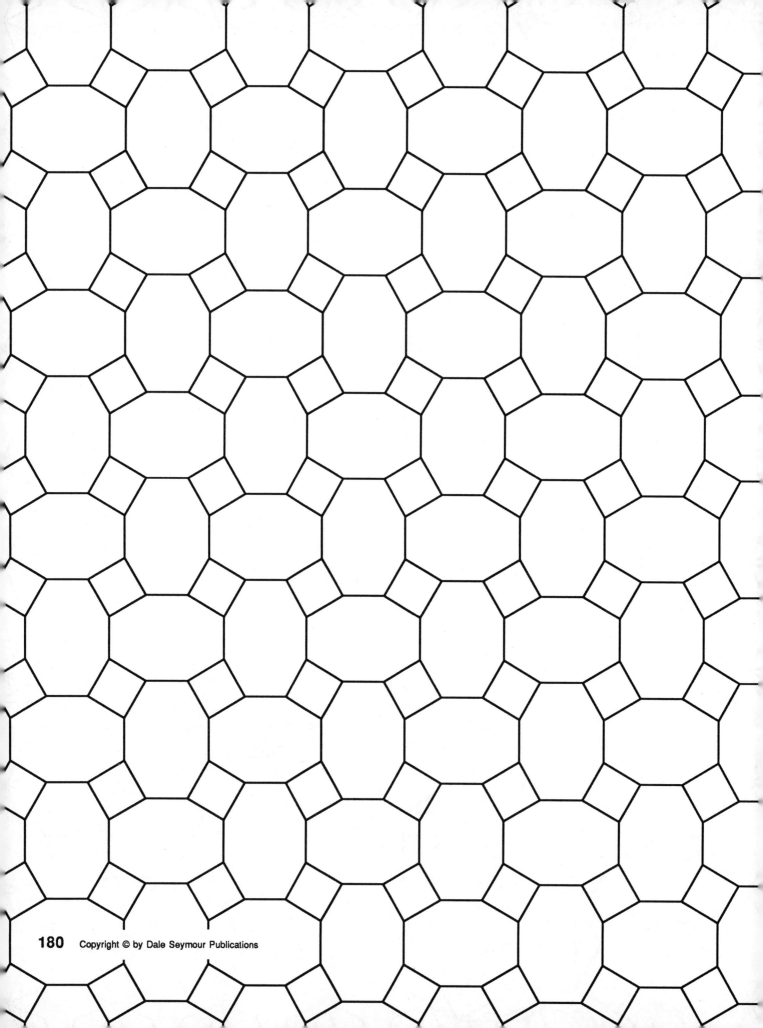

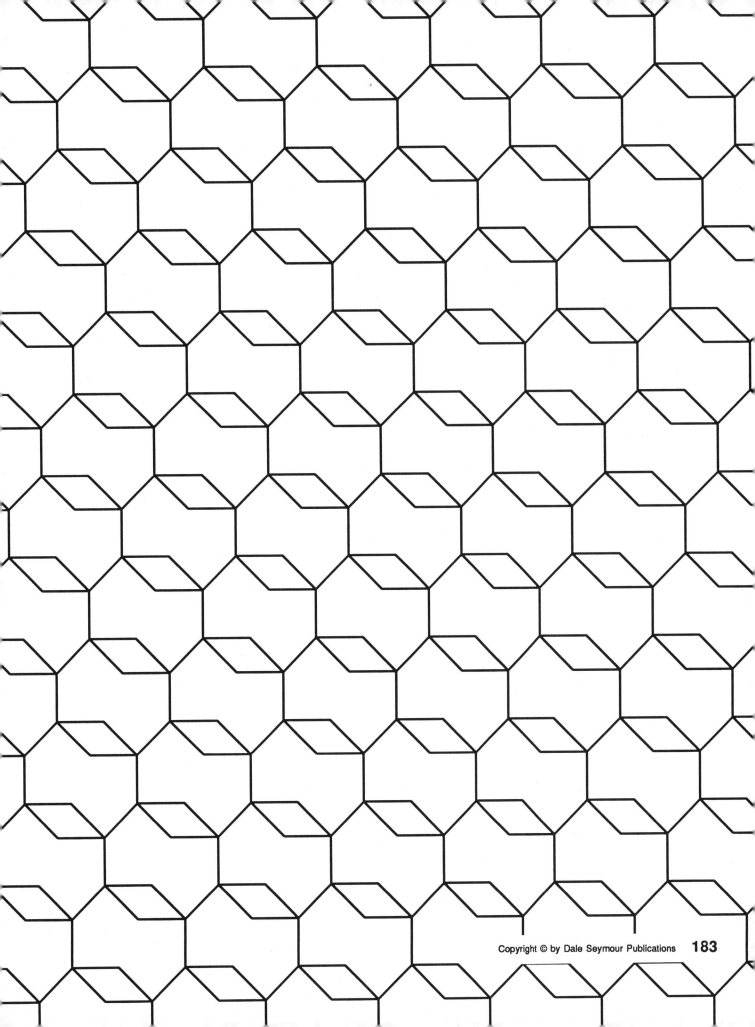

183

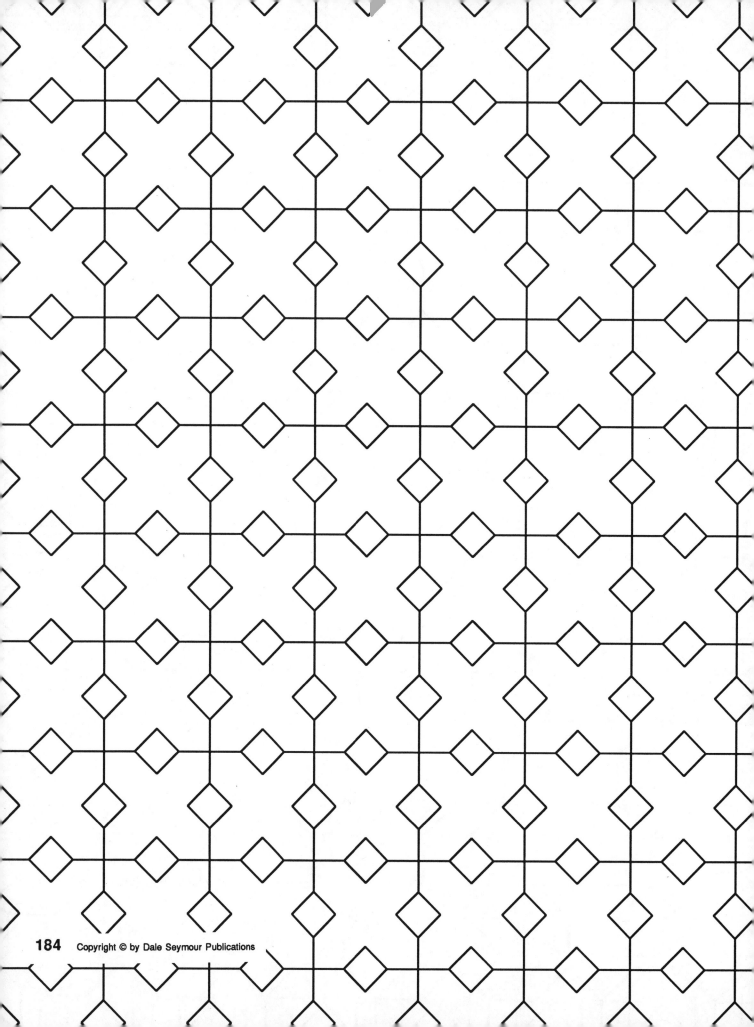

185

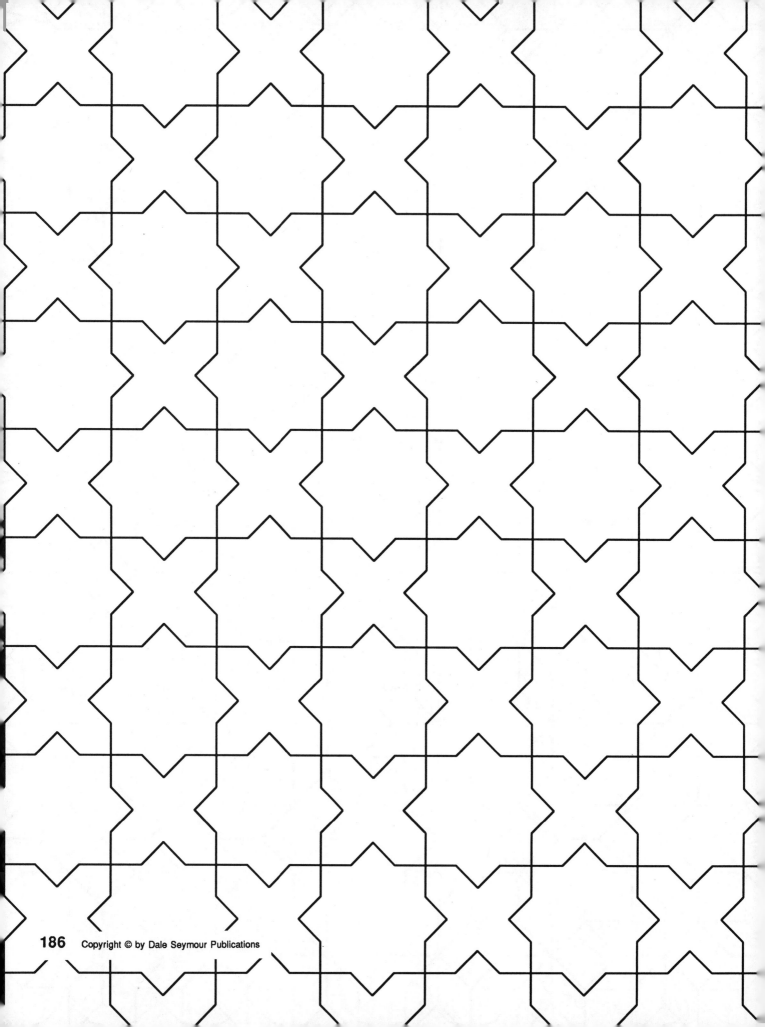

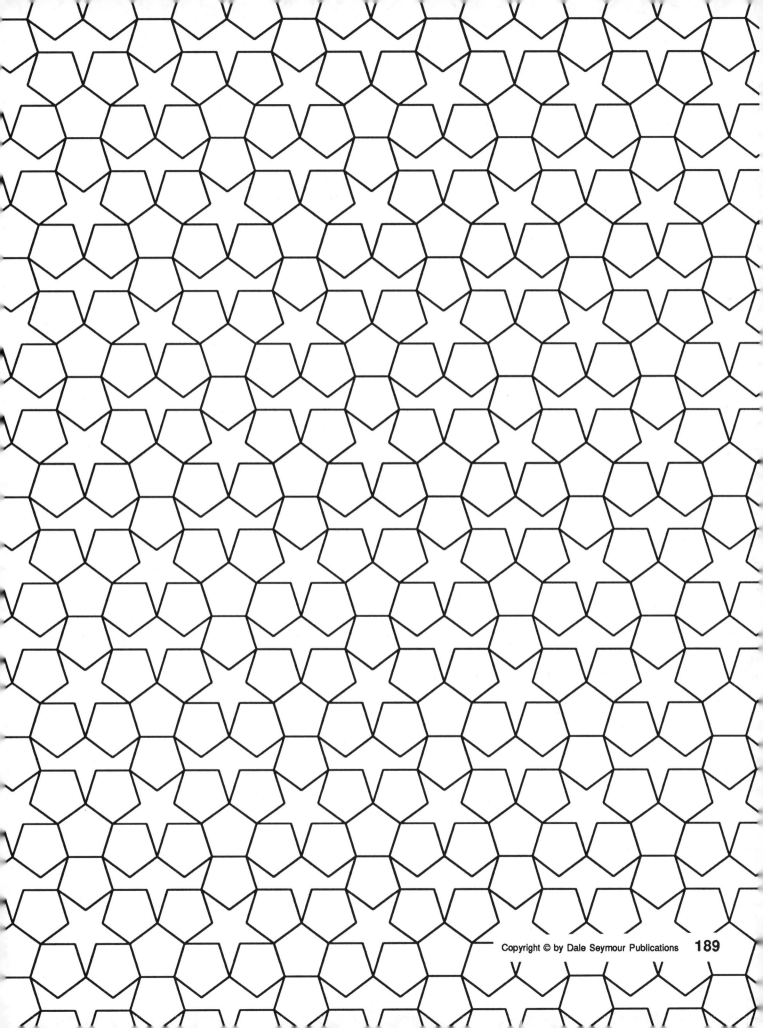

189

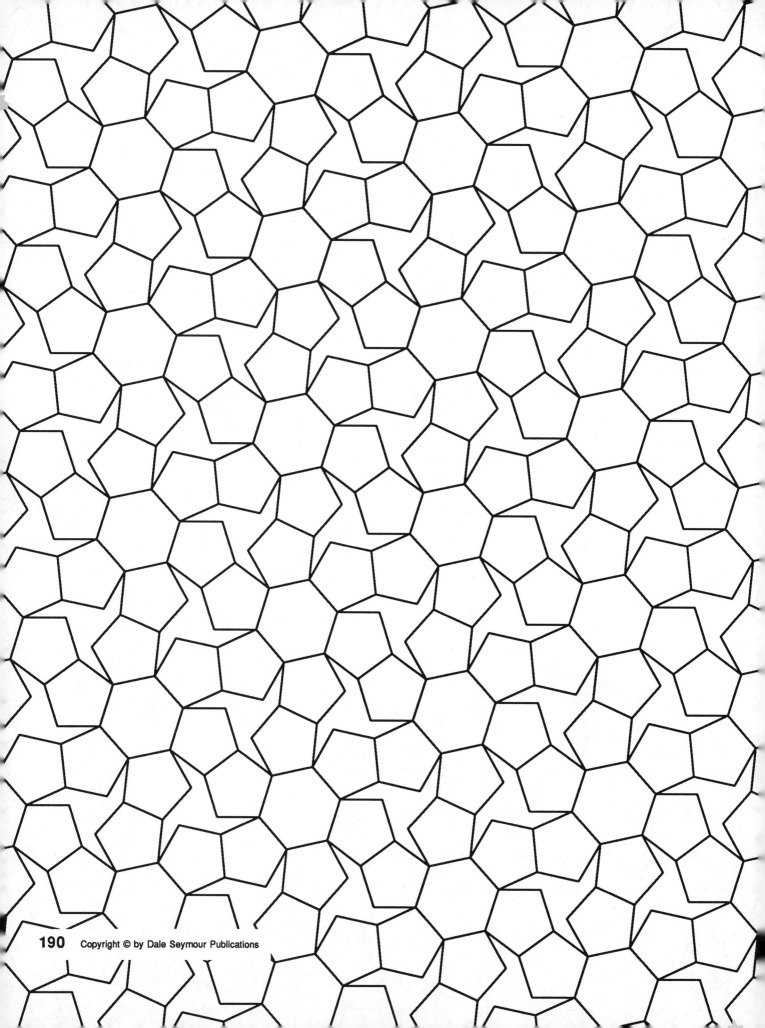

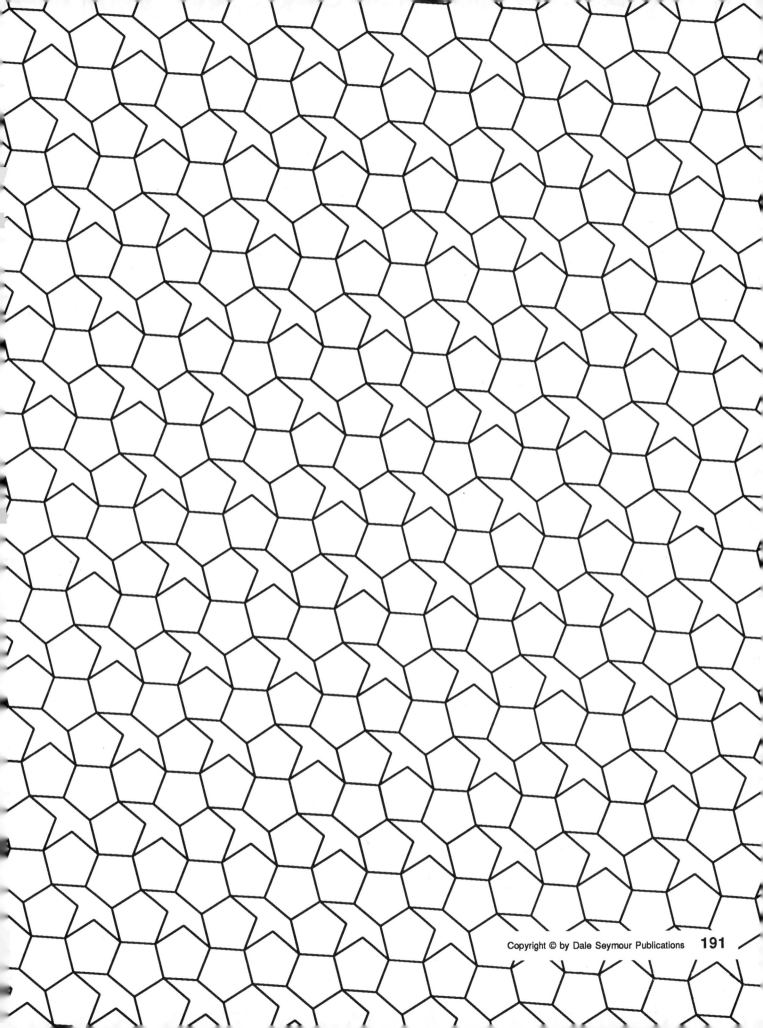

191

193

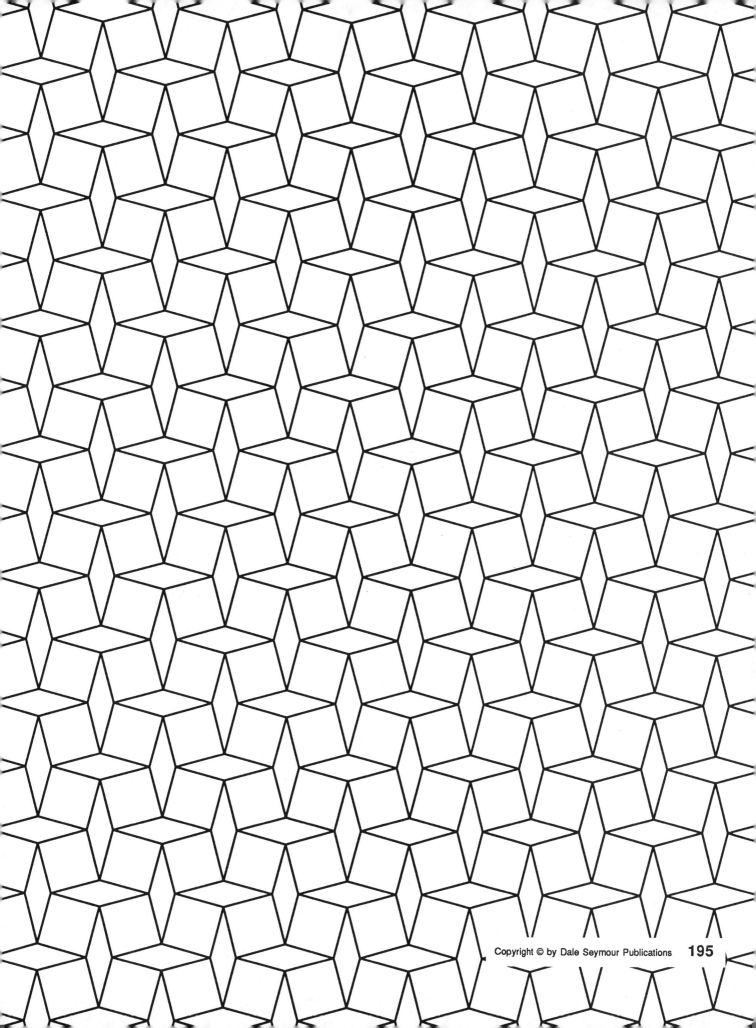

195

197

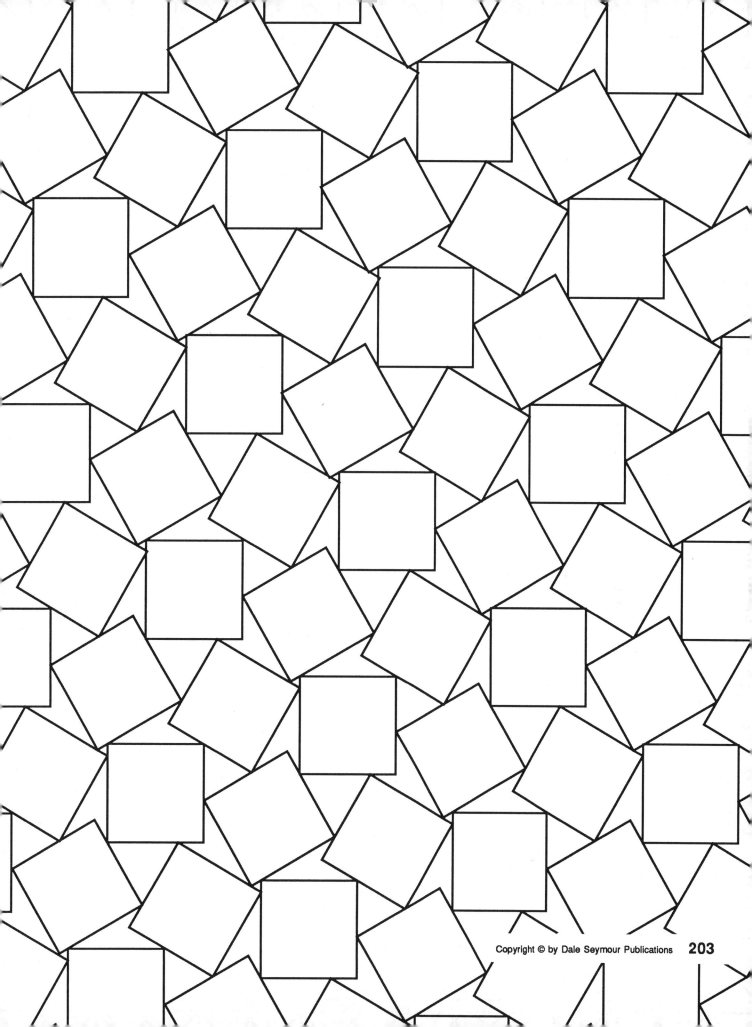

203

205

Sample Tessellations in Islamic Art

209

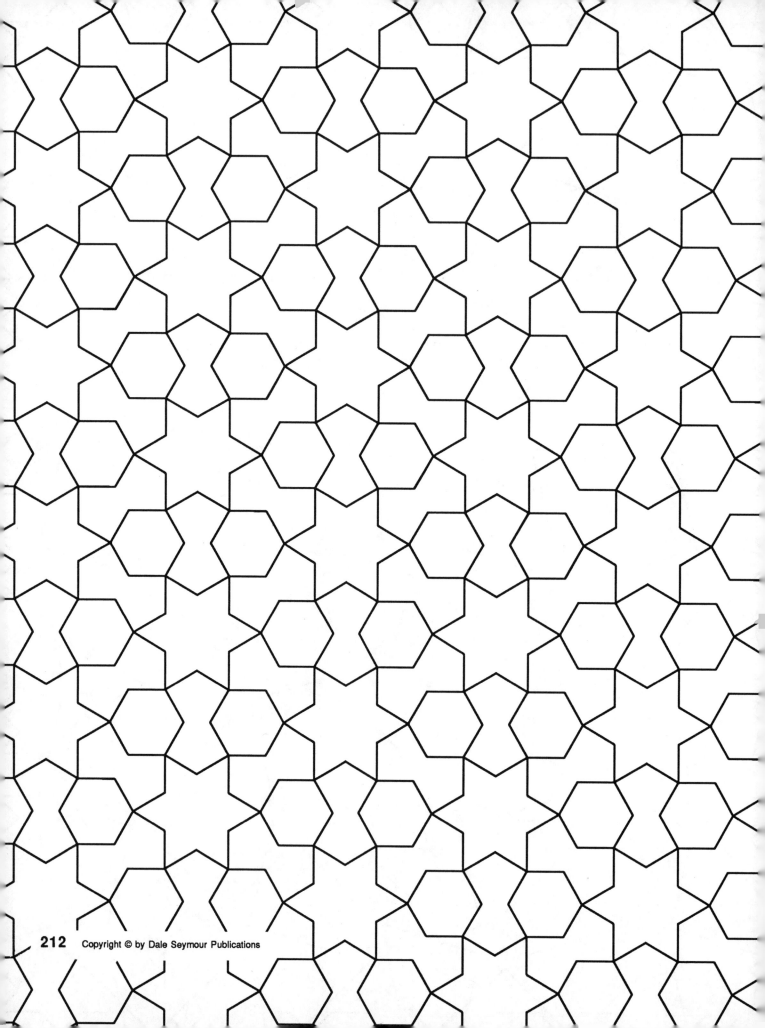

213

215

DUAL TESSELLATIONS

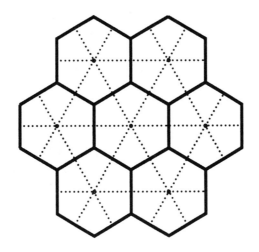

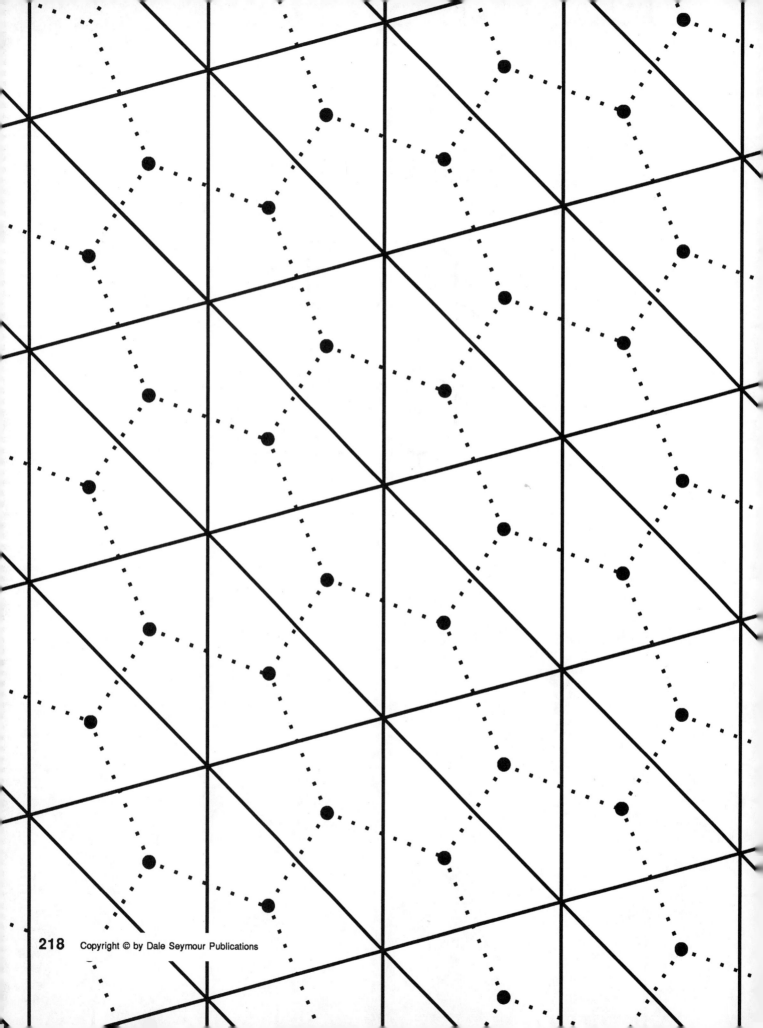

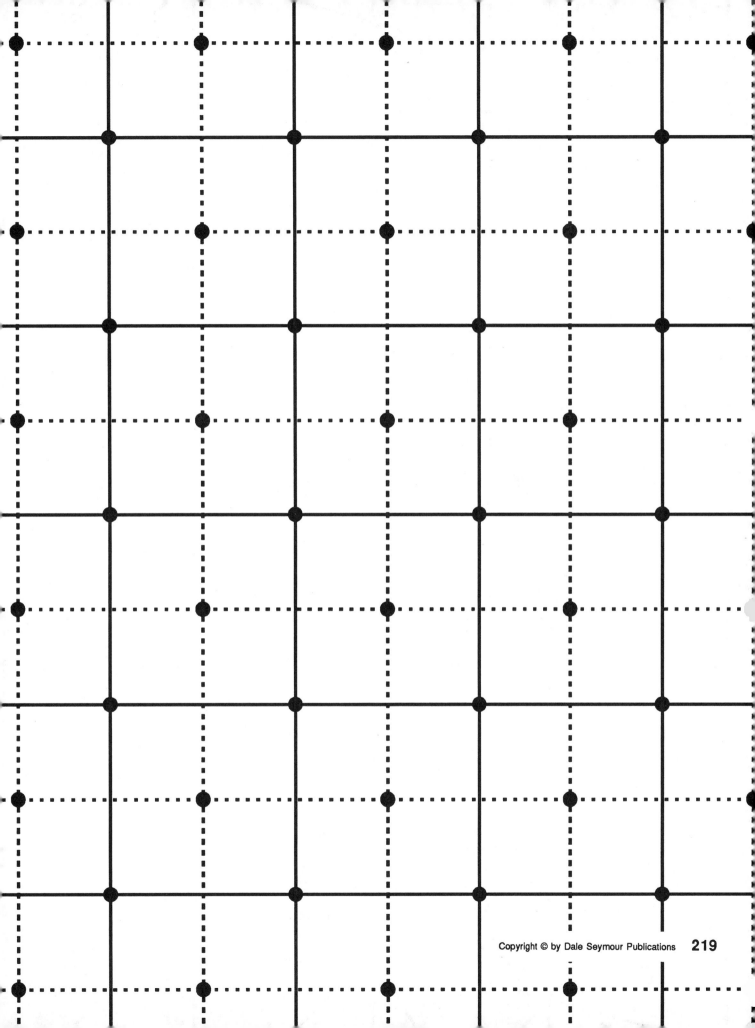

219

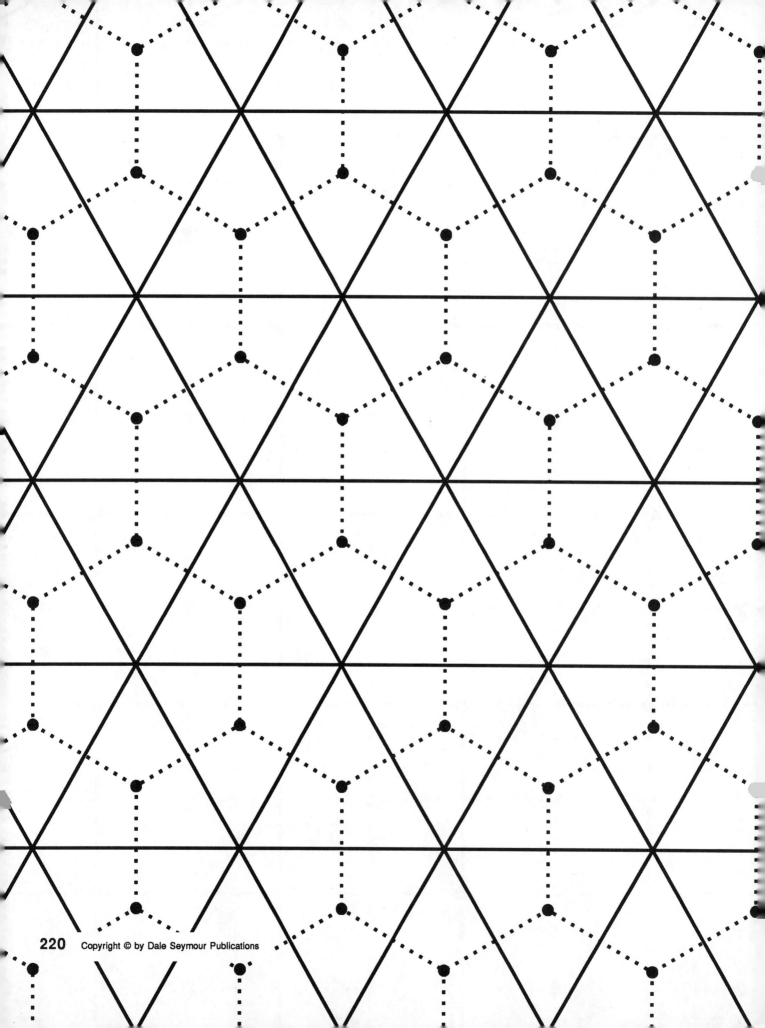

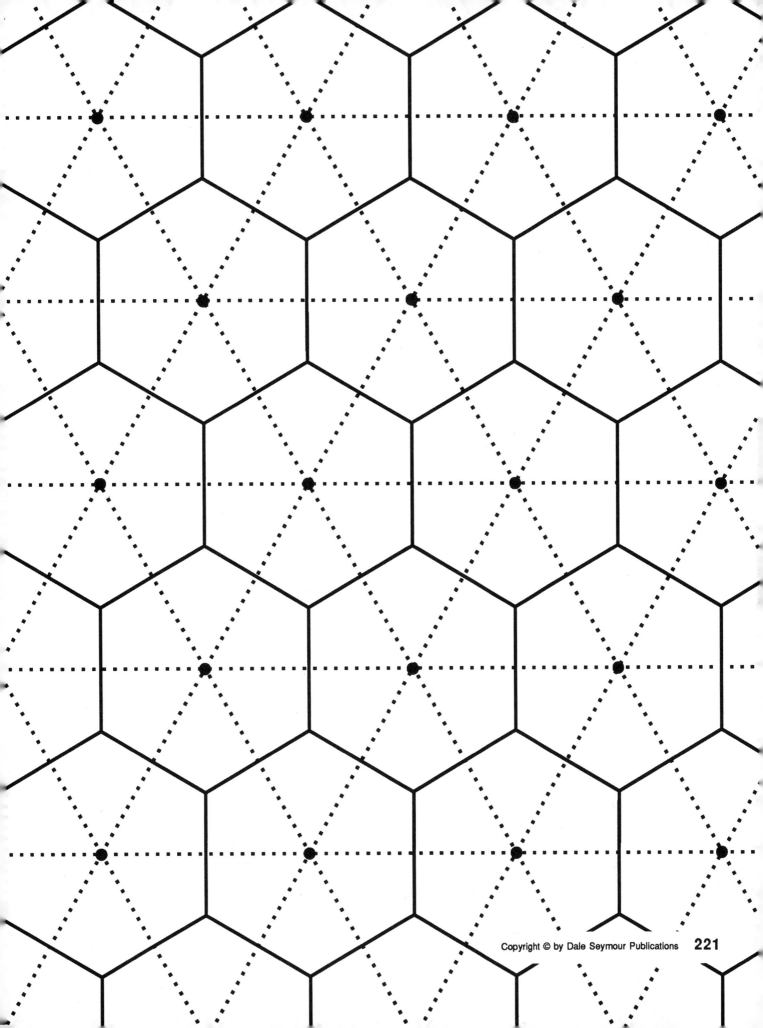

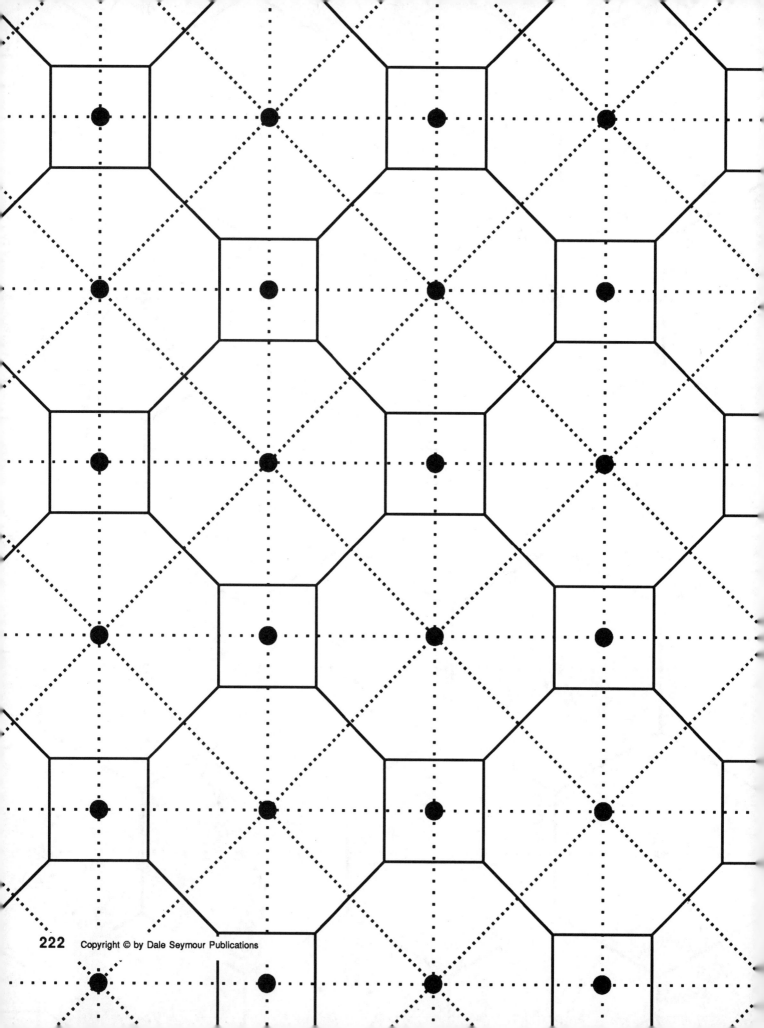

222

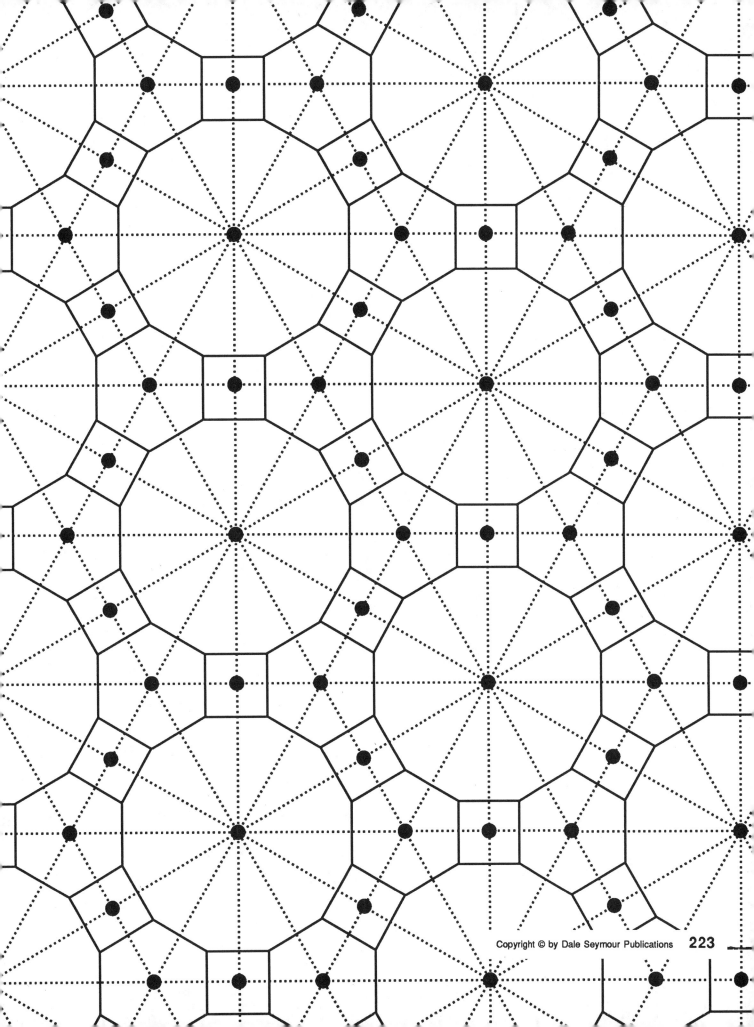

223

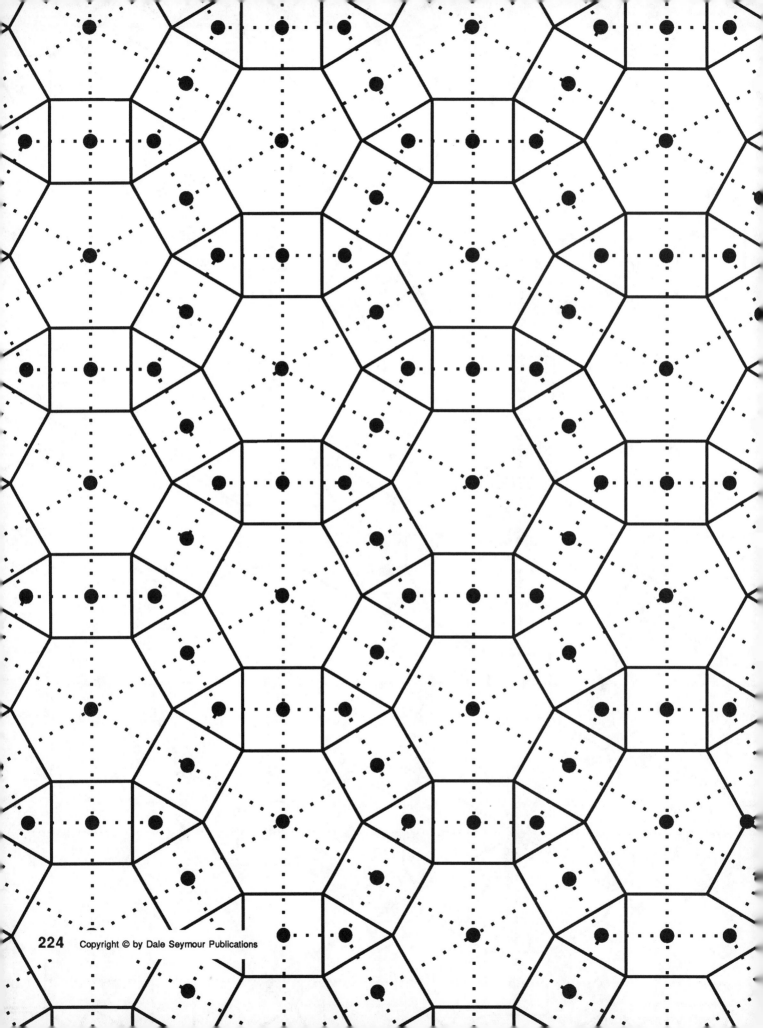

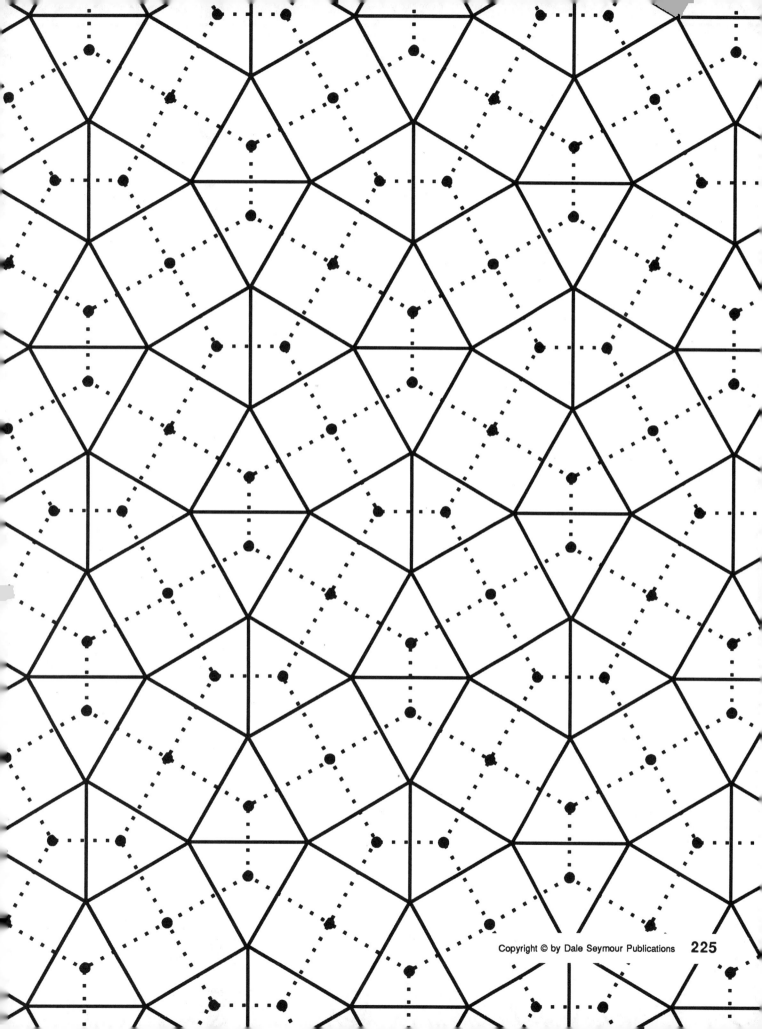

225

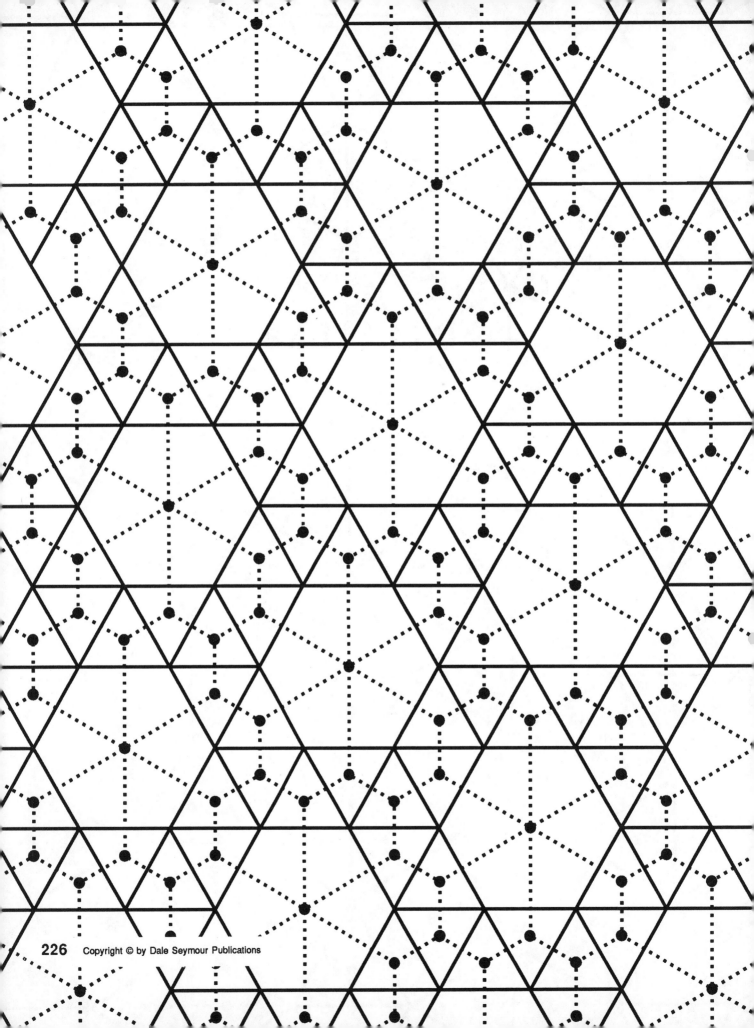

SAMPLE TESSELLATIONS OF POLYOMINOES AND LETTERS

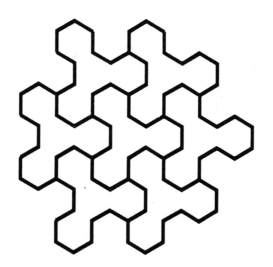

229

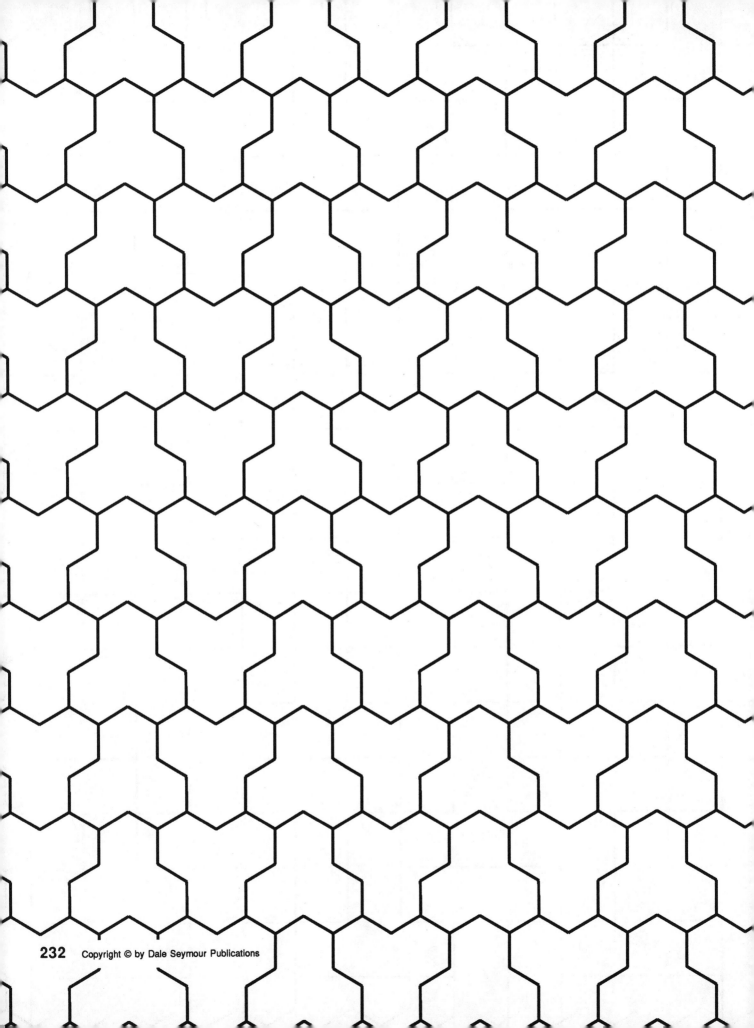

233

235

237

241

242 Copyright © by Dale Seymour Publications

Sample Tessellations of Non-Polygons

244

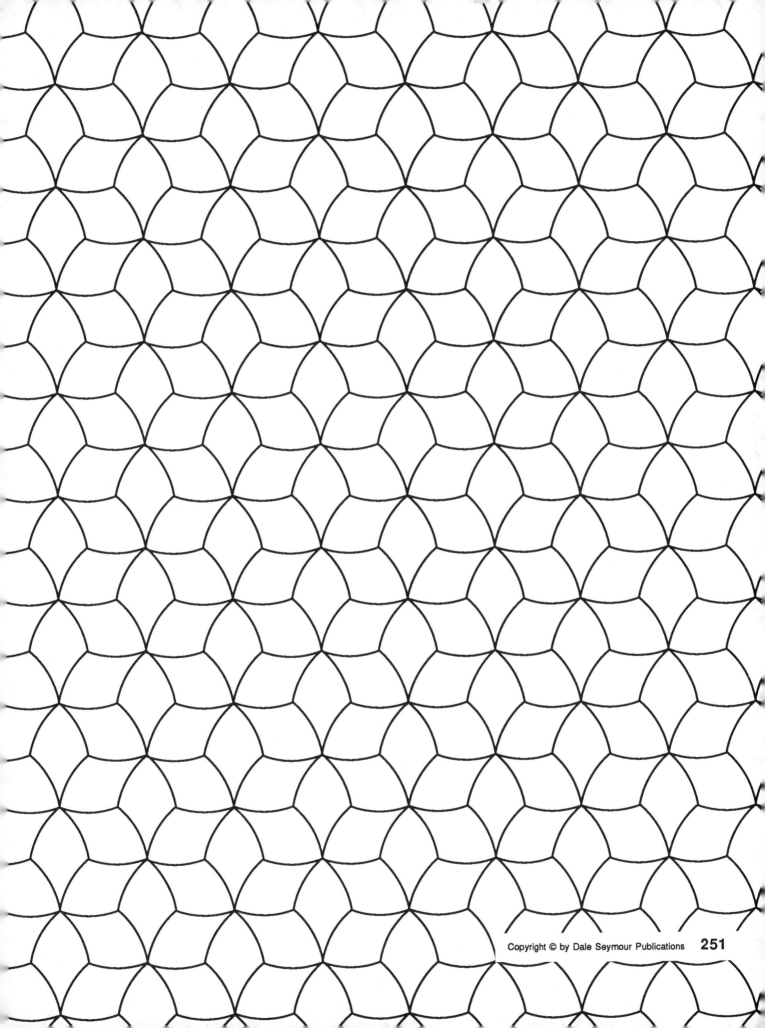

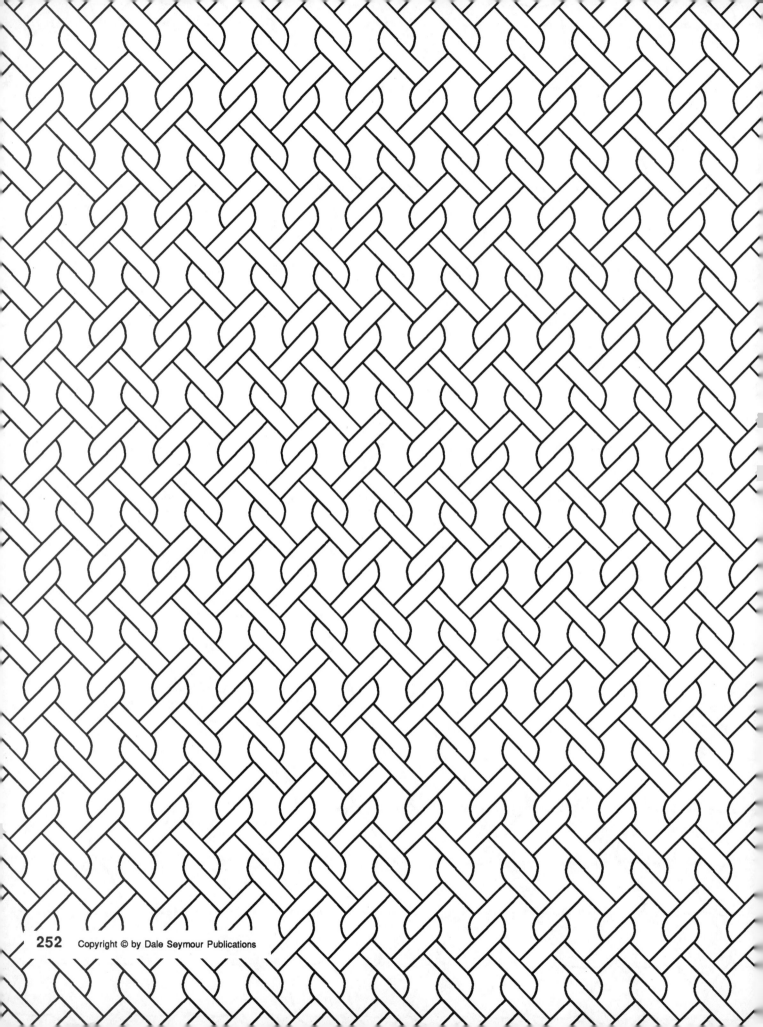

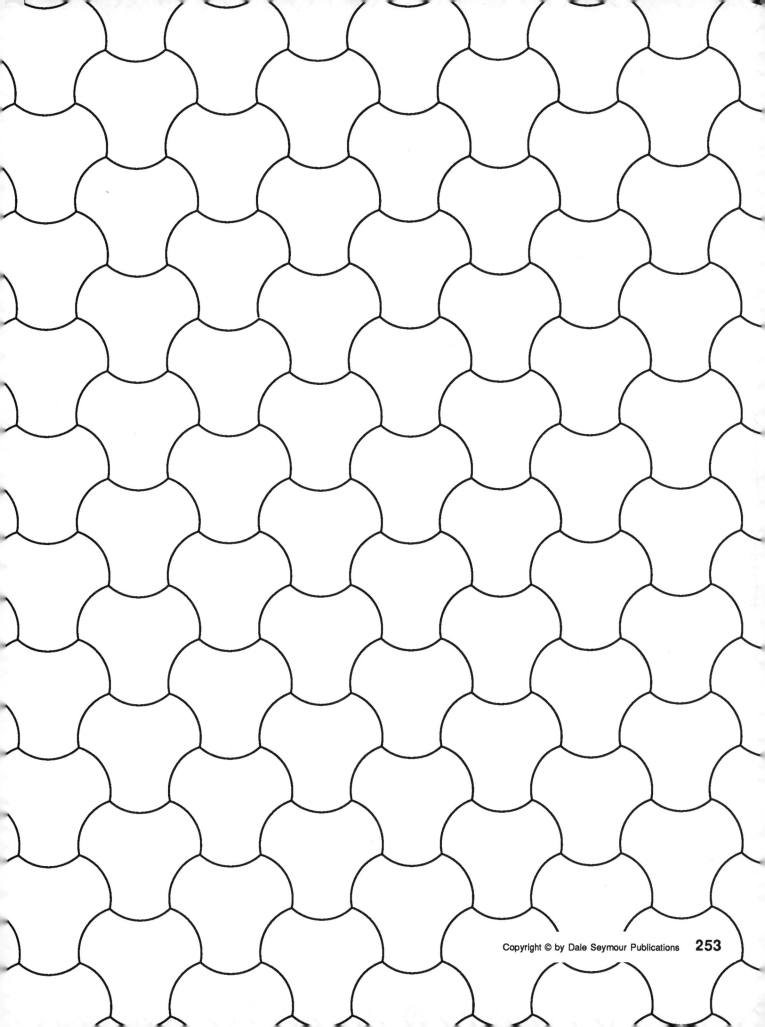

253

254

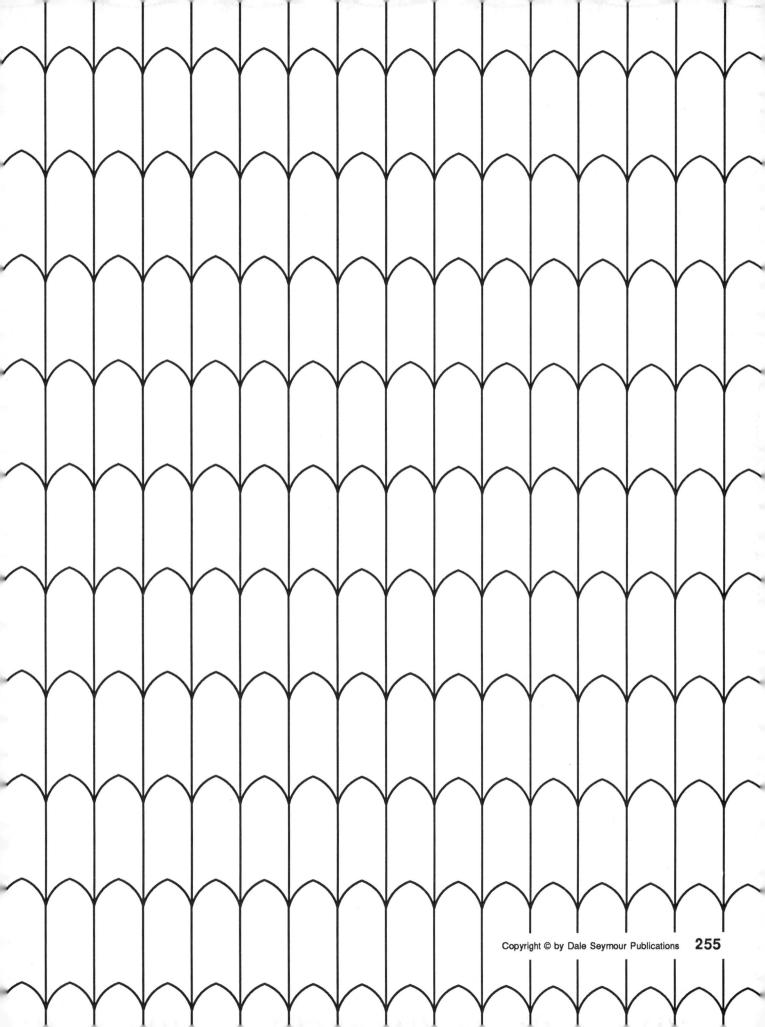

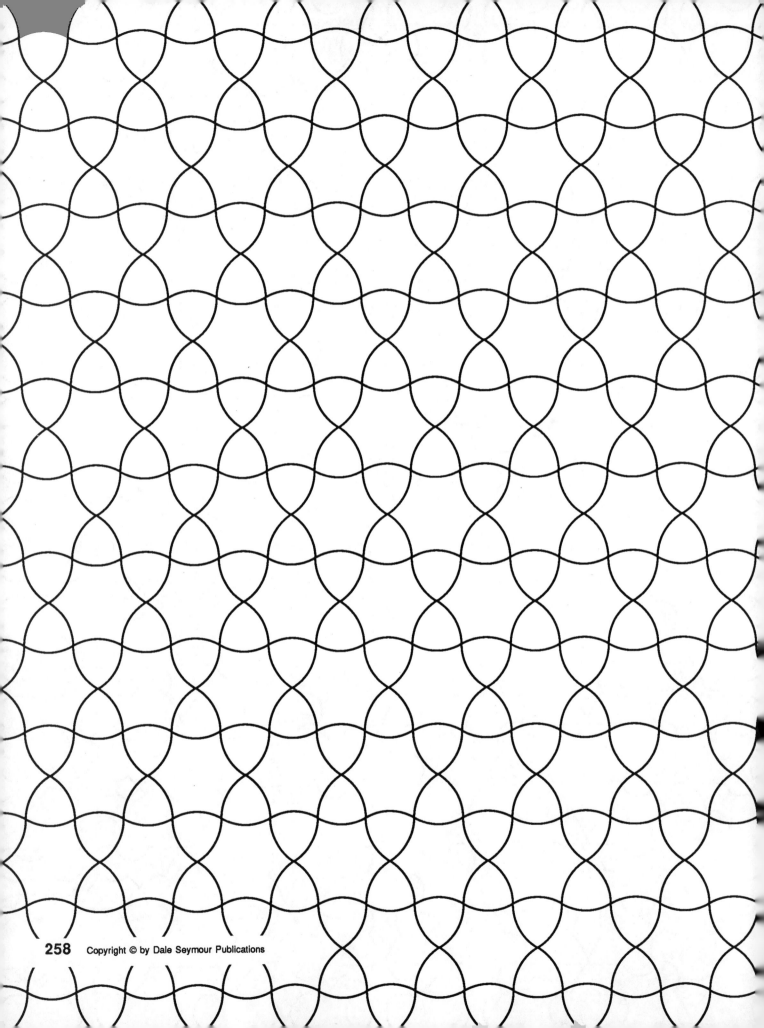

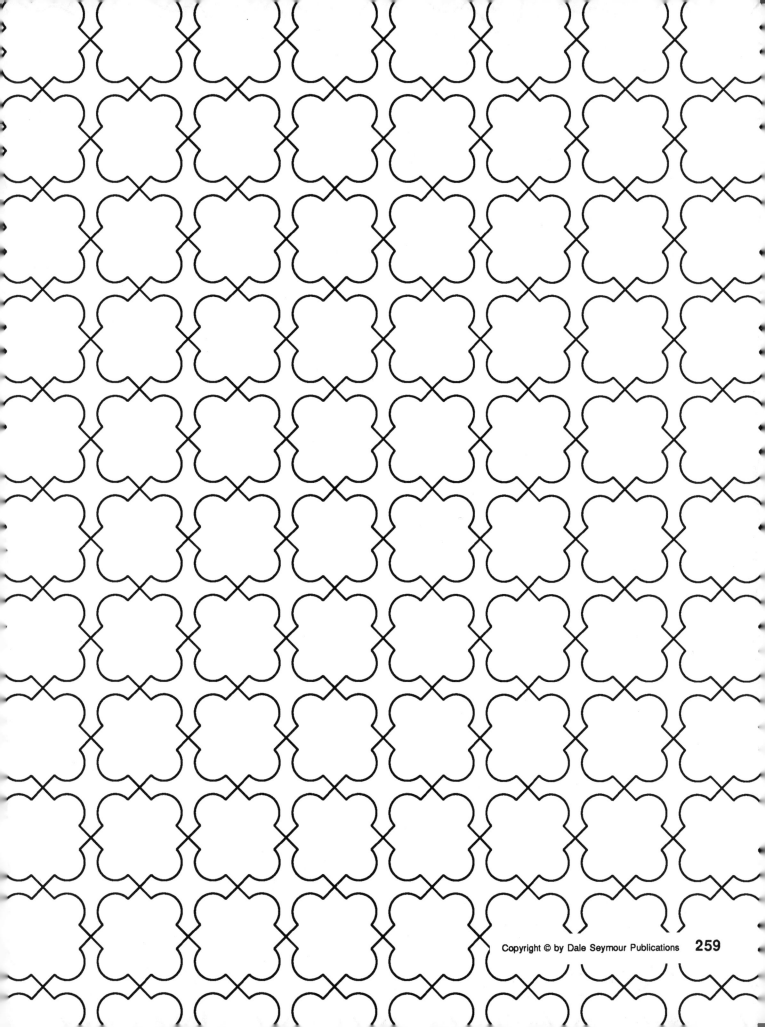

259

SKETCHING GRIDS FOR CREATING TESSELLATIONS

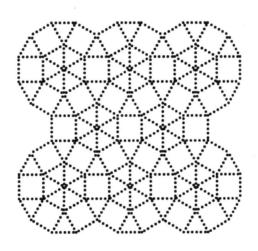

264

266

271

277

WORKSHEETS AND TEMPLATES

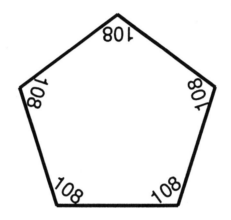

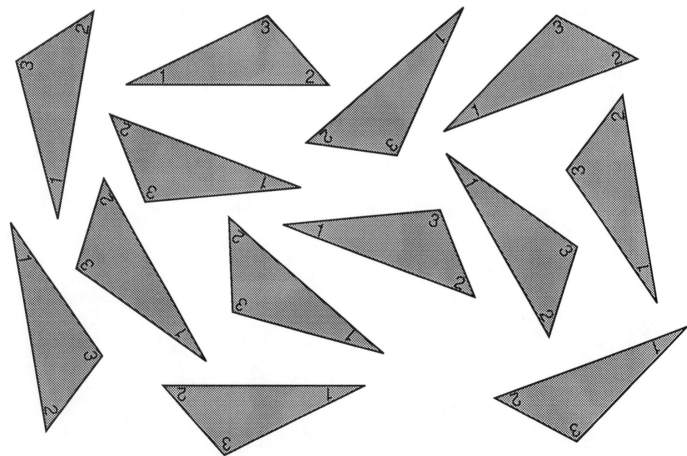

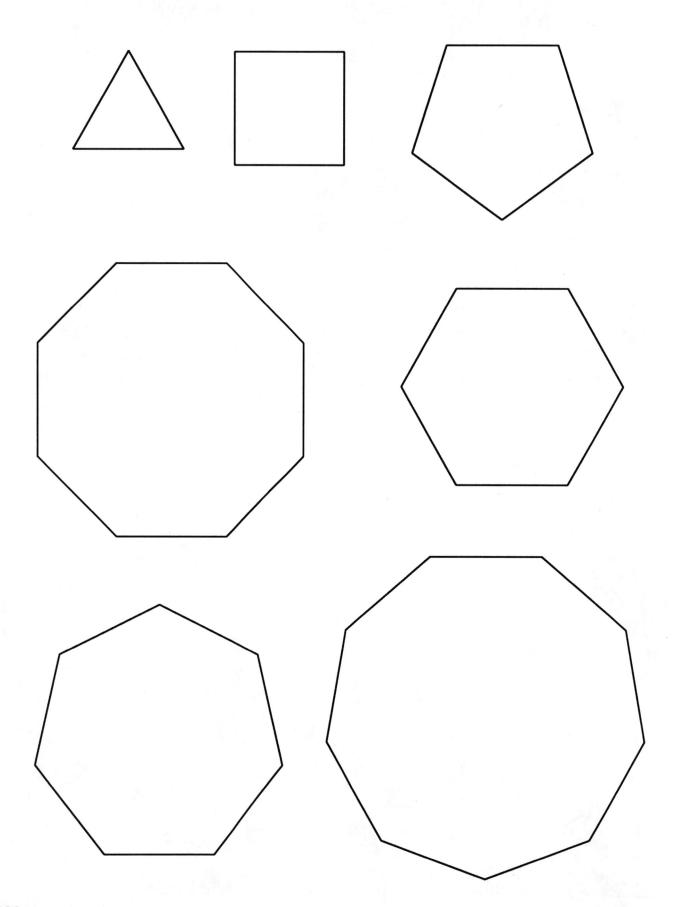

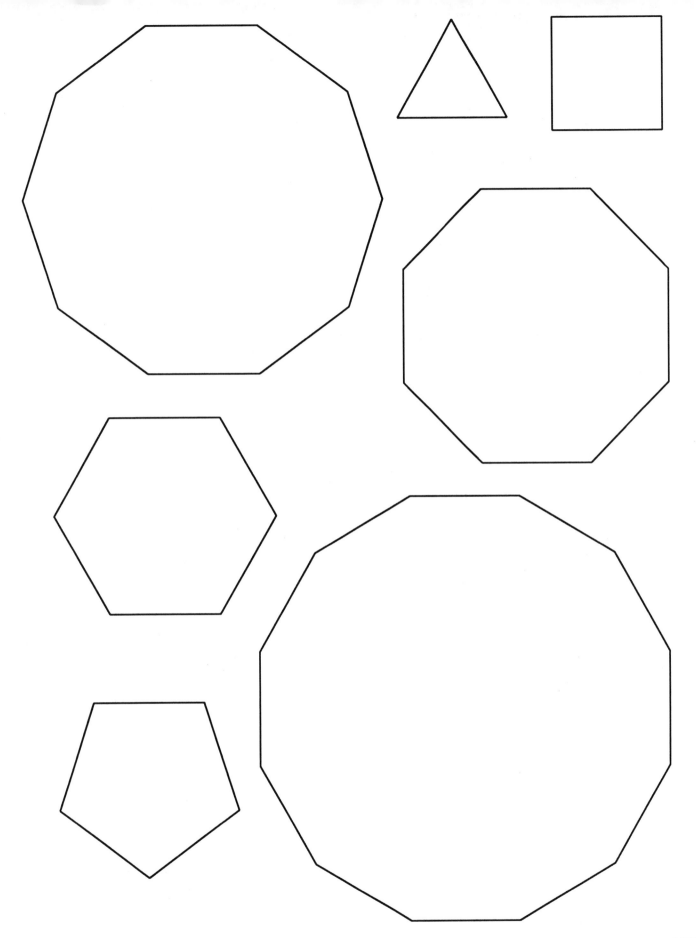

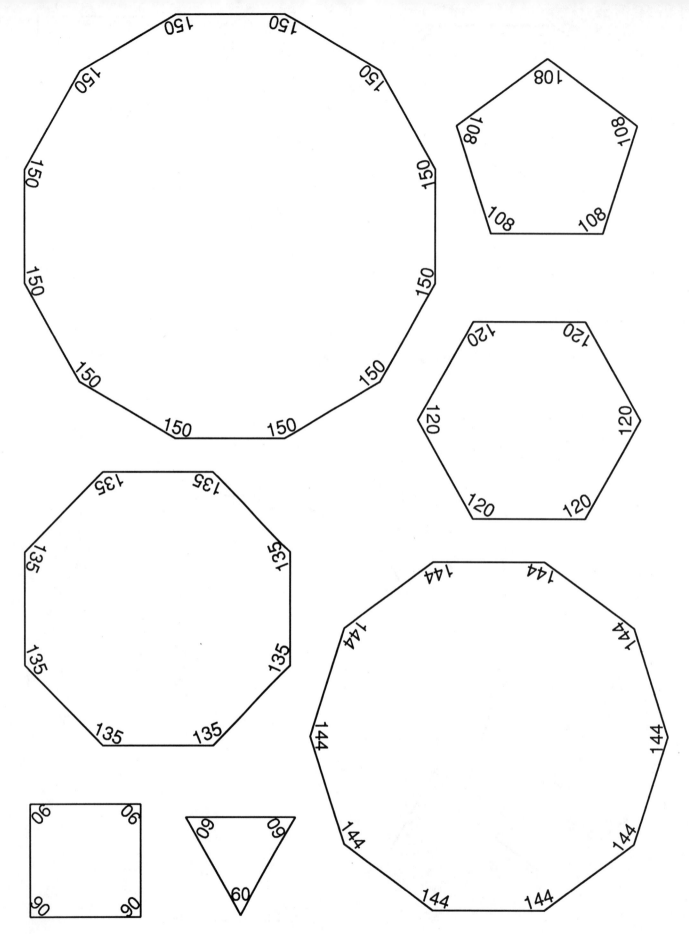

2̄1 REGULAR
POLYGON ARRANGEMENTS

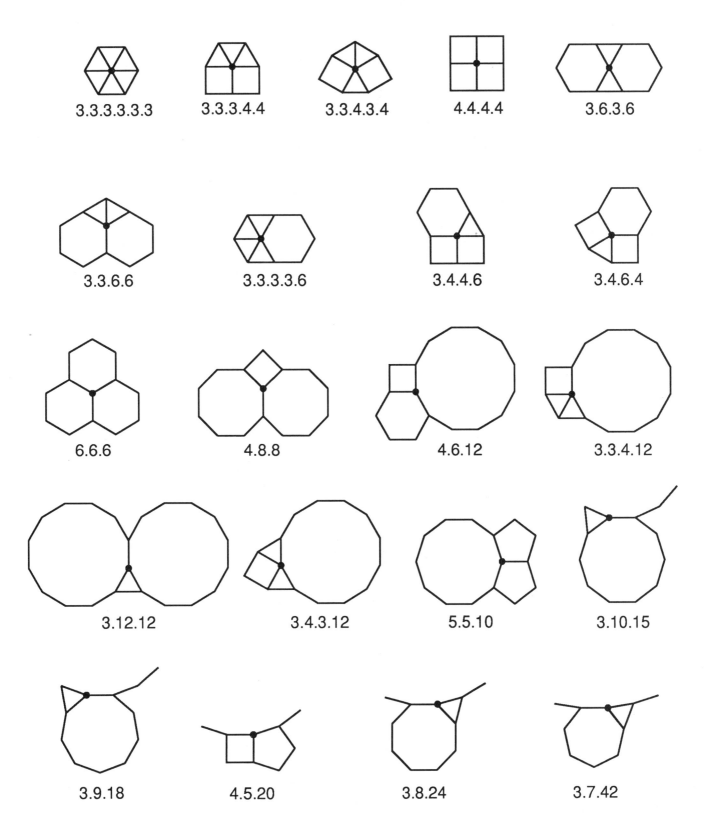

3.3.3.3.3.3   3.3.3.4.4   3.3.4.3.4   4.4.4.4   3.6.3.6

3.3.6.6   3.3.3.3.6   3.4.4.6   3.4.6.4

6.6.6   4.8.8   4.6.12   3.3.4.12

3.12.12   3.4.3.12   5.5.10   3.10.15

3.9.18   4.5.20   3.8.24   3.7.42

285

INTERIOR ANGLE MEASURE IN SELECTED POLYGONS

Polygon	Number of Sides/ Angles	Sum of Interior Angles	Measure of Each Interior Angle (Regular Polygons)
Triangle	3	_____	_____
Quadrilateral	4	_____	_____
Pentagon	5	_____	_____
Hexagon	6	_____	_____
Heptagon	7	_____	_____
Octagon	8	_____	_____
Nonagon	9	_____	_____
Decagon	10	_____	_____
Dodecagon	12	_____	_____
15-gon	15	_____	_____
18-gon	18	_____	_____
20-gon	20	_____	_____
24-gon	24	_____	_____
42-gon	42	_____	_____
.	.	.	.
.	.	.	.
.	.	.	.
N-gon	n	_____	_____

INTERIOR ANGLE MEASURE IN SELECTED POLYGONS

Polygon	Number of Sides/ Angles	Sum of Interior Angles	Measure of Each Interior Angle (Regular Polygons)
Triangle	3	$180°$	$60°$
Quadrilateral	4	$360°$	$90°$
Pentagon	5	$540°$	$108°$
Hexagon	6	$720°$	$120°$
Heptagon	7	$900°$	$128 \frac{4}{7}°$
Octagon	8	$1080°$	$135°$
Nonagon	9	$1260°$	$140°$
Decagon	10	$1440°$	$144°$
Dodecagon	12	$1800°$	$150°$
15-gon	15	$2340°$	$156°$
18-gon	18	$2880°$	$160°$
20-gon	20	$3240°$	$162°$
24-gon	24	$3960°$	$165°$
42-gon	42	$7200°$	$171 \frac{3}{7}°$
.	.	.	.
.	.	.	.
.	.		
N-gon	n	$(n-2)180°$	$\dfrac{(n-2)180°}{n}$